"CRAB IS KING"

By
Bernard Averbuch

**The colorful stories and the fascinating history
of Fisherman's Wharf in San Francisco.
Also some favorite Wharf recipes.**

PREFACE

$\mathcal{T}$he idea for this history of Fisherman's Wharf in San Francisco was originated some 3,000 miles away in New York at the sedate Park Avenue offices of the imaginative literary agent, Mrs. Bertha Klausner, where so much literary history has taken place. It was there also that Bertha Klausner originated and nurtured the best-selling "Never Plead Guilty," the biography of the flamboyant San Francisco Attorney, J. W. ("Jake") Ehrlich.

This book began to grow in the Market Street office-building of the now defunct Italian language newspaper, *Corriere del Popolo,* and was nudged along by such Italian advocates as Ercole Caroselli and Joseph C. Tarantino.

The book idea developed over the years as many of us talked of these stories as we ate our way through the Wharf restaurant menus. Through it all Bertha Klausner persisted.

It has been helped to reality by that bellweather of the Philippine Community in San Francisco, J. T. Esteva, publisher of the *Mabuhay Republic.*

Now it has taken its position in the spotlight of public attention.

Bernard Averbuch

TABLE OF CONTENTS

Chapter 1

INTRODUCTION

*F*isherman's Wharf in San Francisco is located along the city's nothern waterfront, a five-block square section of cosmopolitan character, and has acquired an international reputation as one of the most popular pleasure points along the city's 24 mile shoreline. Along this sweep of waterfront at Fisherman's Wharf is harbored an Italian fishing colony, with its picturesque craft, a score of view restaurants, sidewalk seafood stalls and steaming crab cauldrons.

This area of San Francisco's waterfront is the source of much of the original cosmopolitan flavor of the City. It was here that the City was first shaped and discovered some 50 years after the first voyage of Columbus. Juan Rodriguez Cabrillo, a Portuguese explorer sailing the *San Salvador* under the flag of Spain, is given credit for first discovering the great land locked harbor of San Francisco in the fall of 1542. Cabrillo suffered a fatal accident in 1543, during a return voyage, and the *San Salvador's* pilot, Bartolome Ferrelo, resumed the exploration. Ferrelo charted the waters as far as the Farralon Island, some 30 miles off the Golden Gate.

More than 37 years passed before the next ship appeared off the coast. This was the *Golden Hind*, flagship of the English freebooter Francis Drake, and heavily laden with booty ransacked from treasure laden galleons. He put in at the inlet now known as Drake's Bay, some 25 miles north of the Golden Gate.

The first land expedition to the area came early in 1769 and was commanded by Don Gaspar de Portola, a captain in the Spanish army. He set his expedition's sights first on San Diego where, on June 16, he established the first of the 21 missions the Franciscan priests were to establish in California during the next half century.

From San Diego, Captain Portola set out with a party by land up the California Coast. Sergeant Jose Ortega, the chief scout, and an advance party came to the Ocean Beach area on November 2, 1769, passed Seal Rock and reached the crest of the hill to see before them the great body of water known as the Bay of San Francisco. In the fall of 1770, another party led by Lieutenant Pedro Fages proceeded up the west side of the Bay to the spot where Berkeley now stands.

The Spanish King, Charles II, was anxious to maintain his hold on California and in 1774 another party, under Captain Juan Bautista de Anza, founded the first two settlements in San Francisco. One is the site of Mission Dolores and the other is nearby Fisherman's Wharf at what is now the location of the Presidio.

The present state of California was born with a series of dramatic events. On June 16, 1846, a group of Yankee settlers from the Sacramento Valley took over the town of Sonoma and announced the establishment of the short lived California Republic. Three weeks later, on July 9, United States troops under Commodore John D. Sloat occupied the Mexican Capital at Monterey. Then, on July 11, Captain John B. Montgomery completed the occupation of the northern half of the state by raising the American flag above the plaza at Yerba Buena.

On January 24, 1848, gold was discovered on the south fork of the American River. Eight days later, on February 2, the signing of the Treaty of Guadalupe

Hidalgo ended the war with Mexico and ceded California to the United States.

By the end of 1849, the former village of Yerba Buena, which numbered fewer than 400 people at the time of the conquest, had grown to a city of 35,000. Several years later the Genoese and Sicilian fishermen came to start building the tradition of the present day Fisherman's Wharf.

The first fishermen in the area around Fisherman's Wharf were the Indians. Four tribes lived about the Bay and those along the San Francisco shore were the Costanoans, a group friendly and docile by nature. Before the white man came to California they had developed over the years a simple life of fishing and living by the sea. Each of the streams in the area had its own tribe, dwelling close to their supply of food. River names such as Mokelumme, Tuolumme and Cosumnes all signified the people of that name who lived nearby. Cosumnes is derived from the Indian word, Kos-summi, meaning salmon.

The Indians went fishing in frail boats fashioned from tule reeds and they were skilled at navigating the rough and dangerous waters of the Bay. Their food was fish, mussels, seaweed, or small animals which they either ate raw, or broiled over campfires. Clam shells were treasured kitchen items in Indian homes and the abalone shells and small snail fish were held in high esteem. From the evidence left at favorite gathering places along the shore, the clam bakes and sea food cook-outs of the Indian communities were pretty big doings.

Salmon runs were one of the principal sources of food for the Indians and pungent smoke from the drying racks permeated the air along the shores, the forerunners of Fisherman's Wharf crab pots. When salmon cycles were good, the tribes flourished. The Gold Rush quickly affected the lives of the Indian. Gold mining changed the stream characteristics, so that the salmon runs dwindled and the white population had also discovered the tasty qualities of the salmon. As the whites grew in number, they took more ground and took more salmon, spoiled more rivers and the Indian and his way of life melted away.

All this paved the way for the Italian fishermen. By 1850 came the rapid development of fisheries and the way of the fisherman as we know it today.

The Italians came to San Francisco in 1848 and began to seine for salmon, herring, mackerel, anchovy and smelt. They used the small Mediterranean lateen sail boats called "Feluccas" from which they fished hand lines, beach seines and gill nets. Soon afterwards crabs and shrimps were added to the fishing catch. The crabs became popular because of their tender meat and distinctive flavor. In 1876, the Italian "Paranzella," a double boat bottom seine, was introduced and its use spread along the coast. The steam engine began to be used in 1885, making fishing outside the Golden Gate more reliable.

It was the Italians who more than anyone else helped create the lore and tradition of colorful Fisherman's Wharf, mecca of tourist and natives alike. Part of the romance of Fisherman's Wharf is still the melodic accents of the Italian lanuage, even though most of the fishermen are American citizens and many second and third generation of Italians admit they don't speak Italian. The accents of Southern Italy can be heard along the pier where old timers meet to mend the nets. Amidst the modern world of neon lights and streamlined autos, the oldsters still sit cross-legged mending their nets by hand with long, wooden needles.

Fisherman's Wharf took its present form gradually.

In the early days, North Beach was an important center of recreation. In 1872, the State Legislature passed a bill "to set aside and assign for the sole and exclusive use of the fishermen of the City and County such place or places that shall be deemed proper and sufficient." The 1872 bill approved the cutting of Columbus Avenue through to Beach Street, which was then the shore of the Bay. The fishermen were moved to the foot of Union Street, where they remained until 1900, when the Board of State Harbor Commissioners set aside the present Fisherman's Wharf area for the use of commercial fishermen.

Charles S. Greene best described the Italian fishermen of that era in an 1892 article in *Overland Monthly:*

"Fisherman's Wharf is a bit of Italy deposited bodily in our cosmopolitan City. The boats are moored here in long, double rows, just like those to be seen in the Bay of Naples.

"They do good service, these small Feluccas, sharp at both ends and with a three-cornered lateen sail. They boldly venture outside the Heads, the principal fishing grounds outside the Golden Gate, in weather that would frighten a much larger craft. I have seen them coming in over the inner bar, when it was breaking heavily, and the little craft would seem to stand perpendicular, now on the sternpost and now on the stem.

"But, here they are at rest and their venturesome owners dry and mend the warm, brown nets that carpet the festoon all parts of the Wharf.

"They are picturesque fellows, dressed in gum boots, blue trousers, bright sashes, check flannel shirts and fur hats. Most of them speak but little English and are inclined to be surly with curious strangers. Yet, if a favor is to be asked of them, the sure and swift way to win his heart is to offer him a bottle of heavy, sour Claret that he loves.

"The Italian fisherman is a volatile chap, always eager to sing while his hands are busy mending nets or keeping the boats in snug condition. Often on Sundays, though it is a day of rest, the whole family dressed in their best will swarm over the Wharf, chattering and laughing and singing. The men tinker on board, painting or polishing the craft and getting ready for the Monday morning cruise.

"The Italians usually put out to sea at two or three o'clock in the morning, so as to reach the fishing grounds by daylight. With a demijohn of wine to keep their blood warm, the Italian fishermen go out in all kinds of weather to gather their daily harvest of fish. Then one by one they return to their mooring at the Wharf, with decks and holds piled high with fish and crabs."

Waiting for them at the Wharf would be countless seagulls, all waiting for the breakfast they knew was coming from the discarded fish. Women with shawls over their heads and old men, some with buckets, some with baskets, and some only with paper bags, haggled over prices.

Although the henna colored sail of the old time fishing boats have gone the way of all progress, and given way to gasoline engines, the fleet is still a fitting subject for the artist. Its bright, often gaudy colored boats, the dark, weather beaten Neapolitans, and the noise and smell still make Fisherman's Wharf a vest pocket edition of a sleepy fishing village in sunny Italy. Many of the boats are still painted light blue, the color of the Blessed Virgin, protector of seafaring men.

The Italian flavor is preserved each year by the annual blessing of the fishing fleet at Fisherman's Wharf, a yearly observance since 1935. This colorful ritual is preceded by the procession of the Madonna del Lume (Mother of Light) revered by local Italians as the Patroness of fishermen. In accordance with a centuries-old Sicilian custom, a painting of Maria del Lume is borne from the Church of Saints Peter and Paul on Washington Square to Fisherman's Wharf, where it is displayed throughout the solemnities.

This ceremony is usually held in conjunction with the annual Columbus Day Festival and a waterfront spectacle which includes a replica of the landing of Christopher Columbus—the modern version of which takes place alongside Fisherman's Wharf.

The fascination of Fisherman's Wharf, however, despite the occasional carnival atmosphere of crab derbys and water races, is still the heavy smell of the sea and its products. A few of the more fastidious visitors resent it, but most of them wiff it with a good natured smile. It is a strange and curious odor, the cool, bracing sea air, blended with the hot, acrid steam of boiling caldrons, and the none too pleasant aroma arising from piles of slighted aged crab shells.

But crab is king at Fisherman's Wharf and it was because of the crab that the Wharf became a popular eating place. The crab—and the Wharf—has become a symbol of San Francisco just like the cable cars, the hills and the bridges.

The Wharf began to move ahead in the Twenties when Italian immigrants, and descendants of the original Italian fishermen, began to line the Wharf with huge iron pots, which you still see today, cooking live crabs and offering them for sale to passers-by.

Many of the Italian pioneers at the Wharf started out by working for large fish wholesalers. They were generally paid, not in cash but in fish, which they peddled in wide baskets as they trudged the city's streets, or at

stands they set up at the Wharf. By the 1930s, a number
of restaurants began to supplement the iron pots and
fish stands, and the names of old Italian fisher-families
began to go up in neon lights. These cafes and restaurants
not only featured unexcelled seafood, but distinctive atmosphere.

By the 1940s, the Wharf had acquired a nation-wide
reputation and after World War II an international reputation as soldiers and statesmen from around the world
became acquainted with its flavor and charm. More and
more it became popular to reminisce of "the old days at
the Wharf." Robert O'Brien, a noted *Chronicle* newsman, dined one evening in one of the waterfront cafes in
1949. He looked out onto the waters of the bay, the
lights of the little boats moored under the floodlight
were dimmed, and he wrote the thoughts of an "old
timer:"

"From the top of Telegraph Hill we used to look
down at Fisherman's Wharf. I remember we would see
the steam drifting from the slatted roofs of the smacks—
vapor it was—from the vats the fishermen used to dye
their sails and nets.

"The Felucca Fleet we called it, and more than 100
fishing smacks were there, with bands of red or blue at
the deck line. I remember their sails were brown, like the
color of chocolate, so they wouldn't glare in the eyes of
the men when the afternoon sun was to windward.

"The fishermen wore bright caps and shirts and sometimes sashes of red and yellow to hold up their pants, and
we boys used to look down and imagine ourselves in some
fishing village in Italy.

"Most of them, my father told me, went outside the
Bay, to the banks beyond the Heads, for rock cod. Some
would stay in the Bay for rock cod, taking them off
Alcatraz, Lime Point, Angel Island and the reef by Hun-

(Convention Bureau Photo)

Gulls Eye View of the Wharf

ters Point. Sometimes, in November it was, when the herring were running in the Bay, dozens of them would stay out all night, over across the Bay between Yerba Buena and the Oakland shore. We'd look out of our windows and see their lights like a lot of tiny fires burning in the night.

"There was an open fish and crab market on Thursdays, when beautiful housewives would come out and select the Friday fish from great baskets and makeshift stalls, bargaining, flirting and arguing over prices.

"In the evening, they'd all stand for home and then it was dark on Fisherman's Wharf."

Chapter 2

THE MAN WHO BUILT
FISHERMAN'S WHARF

*T*he man who built what is now Fisherman's
Wharf was a scheming, nefarious, unscrupulous businessman named Henry Meiggs who got out of town with a
vengeful posse nipping at his heels. On the other hand,
he was a most extraordinary, brilliant, stupendous and
eminent genius who created miracles of enduring engineering feats and lives on as a national hero.

Henry Meiggs did not build Fisherman's Wharf as a
benevolent gesture to the City. He built the Wharf to
make a dollar, or more accurately 500,000 of them. Indeed, Fisherman's Wharf was first called Meiggs Wharf,
although the character of the area was somewhat different
than that of today.

When his Wharf was completed in 1853, Meiggs hired
500 men to fell the choicest trees in the forests of Contra
Costa County, hauled them by raft to his Wharf, converted them into lumber at his saw mill there and made
a reported $500,000 in the operation.

Henry Meiggs was a civic and business meteor who
came to San Francisco in the Gold Rush. He quickly
became active in civic and business life and eventually
became a member of the City Council. A lover of music,
he promoted concerts and brought many artists to the

City and built the Music Hall, on a part of the site later occupied by the Occidental Hotel.

Born in the New York village of Catskill in July, 1811, he worked for his father who was a builder of piers and maritime works. Soon young Meiggs went into the lumber business and in 1832 moved to New York to expand his operations. When news of the Gold Rush came in 1849, the energetic Meiggs chartered the ship *Albany*, loaded it with a cargo of lumber and set sail for San Francisco, where he arrived in July, 1849. At once he sold his lumber at twenty times its cost, netting a profit of some $50,000. This daring stroke supplied him with means for future operations.

Meiggs foresaw the city's growth and the consequent certain demands for lumber. He, therefore, sought a place to build a Wharf where ships carrying lumber could anchor. He choose a section in North Beach, which was then less than a mile from the center of the City. The original shore line of North Beach, between Telegraph Hill and Black Point, was a deep cove to Francisco street, from which Meiggs Wharf extended 1,600 feet into the Bay, to the present line of the Embarcadero. It was also near the Golden Gate and land prices were much lower than in the populated districts. Meiggs believed that by proper management much of the growth of the city could be turned towards North Beach. He bought extensively there, with the help of some friends, filled in a number of lots and built Meiggs Wharf.

As a member of the City Council, Meiggs was in a position to do something substantial for his interests in North Beach. He caused several streets to be built in that direction and thus made it easy of access from the business district. These improvements, along with taxes and street assessments, demanded more money than Meiggs could spare from his lumber business. He had expected that his property would increase quickly in value and that he would be able to sell a few lots at a big profit. But, the public was not interested.

From the time he built his Wharf, Meiggs was never out of debt. He had borrowed large sums of money at high interest and consequently was in need of large sums of cash, and finally was pressed for a $40,000 payment. Another blow struck Meiggs in 1854 with a serious business crash and he was dragged down into bankruptcy. But, for the moment he was the only person who knew this. It was then that Meiggs resorted to forgery, and theft, and the City coffers were closest at hand.

San Francisco, in 1854, was doing business on credit, and the notes were paid by warrants signed by the comptroller and the Mayor. As a matter of convenience the two officials signed a considerable number of blanks in advance, and when payment was made the warrants were usually filled out and dated as needed. Very convenient, but very careless.

Meiggs had often used these warrants in his civic duty and now decided to use them to prop up his Meiggs Wharf project and other debts. He borrowed quite a few blank warrants and filled them in as needed. He needed some $365,000 worth, the total number of forged warrants that were later discovered, but even that was not enough. He was in debt to a tune of some $800,000, on which he had to pay $30,000 interest each month.

Meiggs then tried a daring stunt to bail himself out. At this juncture a City election was held and Meiggs succeeded in getting his brother John elected to the office of Comptroller. He had hoped through the election of his brother to prevent knowledge of his forgeries becoming known, though his brother himself at the time was not aware of the forgeries. At any event, the business upturn for which Meiggs had hoped did not materialize and he

The Extraordinary Henry Meiggs

found himself unable to continue the deception until his
brother assumed office.

About the first of October, Meiggs took a good look
at his position and to put it mildly, he was in a jam. He
then got in touch with his old friend, Captain Jacob
Cousins, skipper of the bark *American*. Within a couple
of days, a two-year supply of provisions, including $2,000
worth of delicacies and vintage wines, had been placed
in storage on the ship. Four small cannons were mounted
on her decks. When asked by waterfront idlers what was
going on, Captain Cousins replied that a couple of wealthy
gamblers had chartered the bark for a pleasure cruise to
Australia.

It was midnight of October 3, when everything was
ready and Captain Cousins knocked on the front door of
the Meiggs mansion at Montgomery Street and Broadway.
On a table were two bags of gold, each containing $5,000.
Meiggs pushed one over to Cousins.

"Captain," he said, "this is hell, but I can't help it.
We've got to leave tonight."

Taking the newly elected City comptroller with him,
he got in a carriage and drove to the waterfront and
transferred to a small boat which carried him out to the
American. Minutes later, in the pre-dawn darkness the
bark was underway.

When news of Meiggs' manipulations got around "excited mobs surged about the streets in search of the of-
fender." Vigilante committees in those days were noted
for taking quick action. But, by then Meiggs was well out
to sea. The grand jury immediately returned an indictment against Meiggs and several months later when it
was learned he was in Chile, Governor John Bigler took
action.

Governor Bigler, bypassing the usual channel of the
State Department, wrote directly to the United States

minister in Chile, enclosing a copy of the indictment and seeking the extradition of Meiggs. This was an unusual move that went to the Supreme Court of Chile, for it was the first case of extradition raised in the history of Chile. The Supreme Court approved the arrest and extradition of Meiggs, but when it came time to arrest the fugitive he was nowhere to be found.

In 1857, two years later and by an interesting stroke of fate, Governor Bigler, who had asked for Meiggs extradition, was himself appointed minister of the United States in Chile. Far from being harmful to Meiggs, the coming of Bigler was a positive help and no doubt saved Meiggs. Bigler, a kind hearted man, was disposed to look on the better side of Meiggs life. He had known Meiggs in California and had come under the spell of his personality. At any rate, after Bigler came to Chile he met Meiggs and treated him in a friendly manner. This had a favorable effect on the feeling of Chilean businessmen towards Meiggs, who until then had been leading a miserable life without funds and without business opportunities.

Meiggs' fortunes turned brighter and in the years ahead he carved a phenomenal career in Chile. He built several railroads in Chile and Peru, including one that spanned the Andes, considered one of the world's engineering marvels, and earned a fortune of some $100 millions. When he died in Lima, Peru, in 1877 he was considered by some a national hero, and by others as still a scoundrel because of his business practices in Chile.

Prior to his death he was able to make restitution for most of his indebtedness in San Francisco and in 1873 the California legislature passed a bill exonerating him in case he should return. The bill was vetoed, however, by the governor on the grounds it was an infringement of the executive's pardoning power.

Chapter 3

THE INVASION OF SAN FRANCISCO

*T*he first and only sea borne military invasion of San Francisco took place a short distance westward of the present location of Fisherman's Wharf, at the site of Fort Point, the ghost-like deserted bastion underneath the southern approach of the Golden Gate Bridge.

Captain John Charles Fremont, the swashbuckling empire builder and a most ambitious adventurer and politician known as "The Pathfinder," was the man who led the attacking forces. He accomplished his historic deed on July 1, 1846, at a time when the Mexican empire was crumbling and the Americans were anxious to take over California.

Fremont, a brevet captain of topographical engineers in the United States Army, had crossed the continent with the help of picturesque Scout Kit Carson and an army of 62 men, including six Delaware Indians. He had public orders to conduct a survey of Northern California for the purpose of establishing an overland route to the Pacific Coast, and secret instructions for action in case of war with Mexico. War with Mexico came on May 12, and the secret instructions came with the arrival of Lieutenant Archibald Gillespie of the United States Marine Corps.

Fremont and his men were in Sonoma when the "Bear Flag" revolt broke out and Lieutenant Joaquin De La

Torre and a force of 60 men were sent by the Mexican Government to put down the revolt. After a battle between Lieutenant De La Torre's men and Bear riflemen at Petaluma, Captain Fremont suddenly took command of the rebellion. He marched to engage De La Torre's forces at San Rafael and after a skirmish there, De La Torre's men retreated.

Pursuing the Mexican forces southward, Captain Fremont, Lieutenant Gillespie, Kit Carson and his men arrived at the north shore of the Golden Gate, facing across the waters from the cannons of the old Spanish fortress guarding the shores of San Francisco, then called Castillo de San Joaquin, and now known as Fort Point.

The history of the substantial looking fortress dated back to 1776, when the Spaniard Don Juan de Anza founded the San Francisco Presidio and marked the spot for the fort. The first fortification at the site of Fort Point, then standing on a 100-foot cliff, was completed in 1794 by Jose Joaquin de Arrillaga, sixth governor of California. It was first garrisoned by a corporal and six artillery men and armed with eight 12-pounder guns cast in Spain. Earthquakes in 1808, 1812 and 1813 wrecked the walls and barracks. Rebuilt in 1820, the new fort mounted 20 guns, but still lacked any degree of sturdiness.

The brick adobe walls of the newest fort began showing signs of crumbling anew, as the results of firing numerous salutes of welcome to incoming ships, in addition to warning all mariners that none could enter the great harbor without permission. The fort was not properly maintained over the years, setting the stage for Captain Fremont and his men. Captain Fremont wanted to capture that fort, and he wanted it badly. It meant controlling all of San Francisco Peninsula and the resultant glowing reports of a brilliant military maneuver would help pave the road to the Governorship of California.

It is also interesting to note that in his reports to Washington, Fremont gave the waters he crossed the name of "Golden Gate," the first to do so.

Captain Fremont had no way to cross the waters, but luckily found an American merchant windjammer, the *"Moscow,"* anchored at Sausalito. Skippered by Captain William D. Phelps of Worcester, Massachusetts, the trading vessel was visiting the coast of California with a mixed cargo for the purpose of exchanging goods with the Californians for hides and tallow, which was to make up his return cargo.

Captain Fremont and Lieutenant Gillespie then went to Captain Phelps for aid, and were aghast to learn that Captain Phelps was not aware that war had been declared between the United States and the Mexican Government. Kit Carson, writing in his memoirs, *Adventure in the Paths of Empire,* told what happened next.

"Captain Phelps was then assured by the two officers that war had been declared and that they were acting in obedience of the orders of the United States Government," wrote Carson. "Then, too, because of the risk and hazard attached to capture the fort, Captain Phelps was told he would be entitled to $10,000 from said government."

It was Captain Fremont who made the grandiose offer of reward, a controversial promise that caused headaches in Washington, similar to another payment and promise that Fremont later made for Alcatraz Island.

Captain Fremont continued with the story, as told in his *Memoirs of My Life:*

"Captain Phelps and his boat crew were excited and pleased to aid in the work at hand. I arranged for Captain Phelps for the use of one of his boats, with which he met me at the landing before daylight in the morning.

I took with me 12 of my men, singled out as the best shots, and Lieutenant Gillespie. I had learned that little or no guard was maintained at the Fort. Pulling across the strait of water we reached Fort Point in the grey dawn of the morning. We waded through the surf to shore and scrambled up the steep bank just in time to see several horsemen escaping at full speed. We promptly spiked the guns—14 in all—nearly all long brass pieces. The measures I had taken freed all Mexican territory north of the Bay of San Francisco, from the sea to Sutter's Fort."

That's the way Captain Fremont told it. This is the way Kit Carson told it:

"The fort, El Castillo de San Joaquin, had been first built in 1794 and was humbled by the conflicts of time. There was no garrison and, in truth, none was apprehended."

All the adventurers were writers in those days. Captain Phelps wrote his memoirs under the pen name of "Webfoot" and this is the way he told it:

"From my trade room we had selected such tools as would be needed—such as crowbars, axes, and round files to spike the guns. There were in the fort three brass and seven heavy iron fortification guns. That they were effectively spiked would be attested to a few weeks later by the officers of the 'Portsmouth' for in removing the guns to a new fort on Telegraph Hill they had much trouble in withdrawing the files from the brass pieces, which was only accomplished by cutting them away and inserting a copper screw bolt with a torch hole bored in it."

These guns were mounted with others on the south side of Telegraph Hill to form a battery of artillery, from which the present Battery Street derives its name.

Eight years later, in 1853, Captain Phelps submitted his claim to Secretary of War William L. Marcy for $10,000, pointing out he and his men had accompanied the attacking forces across the bay, with Captain Phelps himself acting as pilot. This was confirmed in a deposition submitted by Fremont. "I have always considered the services of Captain Phelps on that occasion to have been very valuable to the United States," said Fremont. That was pretty strong confirmation and evidence from a man who by then had served both as Governor and then Senator from California.

By an act of Congress, three commissioners had been named to process claims from California. Lieutenant Gillespie, who was then stationed in Washington and had become a Major, was asked for his report. Gillespie remembered the invasion of San Francisco quite differently:

"Captain Phelps did transport a party of men seven miles across the bay to the fort commanding the entrance to the harbor, for the purpose of spiking the guns at the fort. The fort was in a very dismantled condition and could not have been occupied without having been almost entirely rebuilt.

"There was no enemy present and the sole object Captain Fremont had in view was to prevent the use of the guns at some future time. There was no risk or personal danger incurred and the services would well be paid for $50."

That's right, fifty dollars! You would have thought that Captain Phelps would have charged the government fifty dollars alone for the crowbars, axes and round files he donated. The claims commission dutifully ignored Fremont's deposition and by unaimous action agreed to pay $50, and that is what they paid.

The actions of the military claims commission in ignoring Fremont's deposition will perhaps be more understandable with a little more background of what happened following the historic invasion and capture of Fort Point. The following day, ten of Fremont's men entered the City and arrested Robert Ridley, captain of the port. Within a week, Captain John B. Montgomery raised the United States flag at Portsmouth Square and another force at Monterey took formal possession of California.

Fremont wanted to be governor of California. He sent back to Washington some glowing reports of his military success, including the capture of Fort Point, and wasted little time in accepting the appointment of Governor from a political friend.

Meanwhile, General Stephen W. Kearny, fresh from a spectacular military victory in Mexico, had entered California with official orders to establish a new government. This led to a conflict of authority and the General told Fremont to quit and get out. Fremont, who was a strong student of history, felt he deserved the title and disregarded General Kearny's orders. The General wrote to Washington and in plain language wanted to know who was boss. Washington confirmed General Kearny's authority and he promptly had Fremont arrested and removed from office. Heaping further indignities, Fremont was tried by a court martial in Washington for his insubordination and in January, 1848, was found guilty of mutiny, disobedience and conduct prejudicial to military discipline. You would think those charges enough to get someone hanged and quartered, but the only penalty voted was that Fremont be dismissed from the Army. President James K. Polk reviewed the case, as military protocol required, and approved the verdict, but remitted the penalty. Fremont, in a bitter mood, resigned anyway.

You can see that Fremont was not the most popular man in Washington at that time.

That was not the end of Fremont. He made certainly one of the most remarkable comebacks in political history. From that low point of disgrace, Fremont's career rose spectacularly and in less than ten years, in 1856, he was nominated for President of the United States by the then new Republican Party. And one of the big factors in his nomination was his popularity for his role in the conquest of California. However, Fremont was defeated in the election by James Buchanan.

After his court martial, Fremont returned to California to establish his home on a 40,000 acre estate he bought near Mariposa. In a short while came the discovery of gold in California and rich ore veins were found on Fremont's estate and he became a millionaire several times over. He was elected for a short term as one of the first two Senators, but was defeated for re-election in 1851. After the Civil War began, Fremont rejoined the Army as a major general, and was placed in command of the Western Department, with headquarters in St. Louis, Missouri. He wanted to free Missouri slaves and confiscate property of those in rebellion, but Missouri was a border state and these were not popular views. President Abraham Lincoln had Fremont removed from his command, after which Fremont retired from public life. In 1878, after losing his fortune, Fremont welcomed an appointment as Governor of the Arizona territory until 1883. He died in New York City in 1890.

After the conquest of California, the conquering Americans realized the site of the old Spanish fortress at Fort Point was the key to the defense of the harbor, as Captain Fremont proved, or disproved. To replace the crumbling castillo they dynamited away the 100-foot cliff to secure a proper foundation and built a more proper impregnable fort. Because of the dribble of appropriations, construction stretched over the greater part of a decade and was finally finished in 1861, and was garrisoned by two companies of the old Third Battalion. The new fort was officially named Fort Winifield Scott in 1882, but in general usage it has always retained the name of Fort Point.

The fort, which is still standing, is a partial replica of Fort Sumter, and has been described as "one of the finest examples of military architecture in the United States." It is a rough quadrangle, 250 feet long, 150 feet wide and 54 feet in height, with walls four feet thick. The three-tiered structure, built entirely of brick and trimmed with granite finished to size in China, surrounds a court yard and a parade ground.

The original armament included 149 guns, which revolved to shoot anywhere in the bay. It was built to withstand long sieges and store rooms there could cache enough rations for 600 men to last four months. Ammunition storage magazines have walls four and five feet thick. The fort was heavily manned during the Civil War when it was thought the British might take advantage of hostilities to capture California, but they never tried, though they did send a fleet to Pacific Waters.

One of the original engineers, who helped build the fort, was Curtis Lee, who was assigned to San Francisco after graduating at the head of his class at West Point. He was the son of Robert E. Lee, and resigned to join his father in the Confederate forces. The commander of the fort, General Albert Sidney Johnson, also resigned to join the Confederate forces and was killed at Shiloh.

The fort was declared to be obsolete in 1905 and its batteries were finally abandoned in 1914. During World War I the fort housed a number of German prisoners and in World War II the fort housed an anti-aircraft unit and anti-submarine guns. In the following years the fort was abandoned completely and its cannon distributed to various army posts that wanted them for display. Two of these guns today flank the Presidio Officers Club, two others adorn the Presidio and two are at nearby Fort Mason.

It was assumed the fort would be demolished for the construction of the Golden Gate Bridge in 1933, however, Chief Engineer Joseph B. Strauss had a fine sense of history and appreciated the dramatic contrast between the rust-gathering fort and his modern steel bridge. He decided to preserve the fort in hopes it would become a historic landmark, which finally seems ready to occur in 1969 with proper legislation introduced in Congress. His assistant, Clifford E. Paine, designed a steel arch to overlap the fort, contrasting with a concrete arch on the Marin side of the bridge.

Fort Point's abandoned condition and aura of mystery and ghost like appearance, has made it an ideal location for motion pictures and television scenes. It was frequently used in the "Lineup" television series. In the movie "Vertigo," Kim Novak took a header off the sea wall and was rescued by Jimmy Stewart, under the direction of Alfred Hitchcock. In order to avoid losing his stars in the raging currents of the Golden Gate, Hitchcock shot the close-ups in a warm water tank in Hollywood.

Historians someday must speculate on what Captain Fremont would have thought of that!

Chapter 4

WRECK OF THE RIO DE JANEIRO

*"The Italian fishermen were first to the rescue
and to the heroic and prompt action of these
hardy toilers of the sea many of the passengers
and crew owe their lives."*

Page One
San Francisco *Examiner*
February 23, 1901

*T*he morning of February 22, 1901, was heavy
with fog and the line of fishing boats from Meiggs Wharf
was chugging its way towards the Gate as the time neared
5:30 o'clock in the chilly dawn. Santos Costa with Matteo
de Jenaro aboard the *"Newcomer"* pulled their oilskin
coats tighter. They glanced back to see Antonio Silva in
his launch, and behind him the handsome, mustached
Antonio Venturini and Alberti Gibelli in the *"Andrea
Doria."* Off in the fog they knew the other paisanos were
there, Andrew Adami, Fred Castarani, Alberto Guino,
Adam Andrea, Matteo Mirabelli, Spono Domini and the
others.

"All of a sudden we heard cries for help," as Matteo
de Jenaro told it later in his Genoese dialect. "Santos
yelled at the others to come this way. Pretty soon we
hear a lot of excitement."

Antonio Silva spotted three men clinging to a raft. He swung over hard and saw one was badly hurt. The tide carried him to shore as he worked feverishly to get the men aboard. Silva then headed his boat to the nearby Bakers Beach Life Saving Station, tied up quickly and rushed inside for aid and excitedly spilled out his story in part English and part Genoese.

The captain on duty quickly spread the news and the alarm, that the 3,548 ton barkentine rigged iron screw vessel, the *City of Rio de Janeiro,* with 211 passengers on board returning from the Orient, had crashed into the rocks of Fort Point, at the shore of the City proper. It was to become the greatest shipping disaster in the history of San Francisco Bay and the source of its most persistent legend that exists to this very day. Before that day had ended, 131 of the passengers and crew had lost their lives, and of the 80 saved most were pulled out of the water by the Italian fishermen.

The story was soon pieced together. All across the Pacific the *Rio de Janeiro* had fought head winds and heavy seas and she was two days behind schedule. The *Rio* always seemed to be in difficulty. Three times before in the China seas she had narrow escapes and on one occasion had to be beached to avoid destruction. She had no trouble in her first runs, between New York and Rio de Janeiro, but in 1895 while off the coast of Japan she ran into a typhoon and struck a sunken rock, tearing a large hole in her side. In 1898, she had collided with the British steamer *"Bombay"* in Hong Kong Harbor. It was with anticipation, therefore, that the passengers crowded the rails at mid-morning of February 21 as the *Rio* hove into sight of the mainland. The passengers were a mixed lot of English, Chinese and Japanese, for fully half of the passengers were from the Orient.

Among the noted passengers were Professor I. Wada of Yokohama, on his way to take graduate work in chemistry at John Hopkins University, and Dr. Onkawara, a noted physician in Honolulu who was traveling with his wife to the University of California for graduate studies. The most prominent passengers were Rounsevelle Wildman, 36, a native of San Francisco and U.S. Counsel General in Hong Kong. Wildman sent the first dispatch to the United States Government of the news of the destruction of the Spanish fleet in Manila Bay by Admiral Dewey on May 1, 1898. A personal friend of Admiral Dewey, he had been given a pennant of the Spanish flagship by Dewey as a memento of the victory.

Wildman was returning with his family to attend the inauguration of President McKinley. His family included his wife, the daughter of a San Francisco judge and niece of a United States Senator, and two children, Rounsevelle Jr., 8, and Dorothy, 2. The counsel was looking forward to meeting old journalism friends as well, for he had been part owner and editor of the *Overland Monthly* in San Francisco for a number of years. Before that he had been editor of the Boise, Idaho, *Statesman*.

Another passenger of some note was Russell Harper, 23, a native San Franciscan and English editor of a Japanese language newspaper in Yokohama. He was coming home to visit his family.

If the language of some of the passengers was strange, that of the crew stranger yet. It was a mixture of pidgin English, for the entire crew of 84 men, with the exception of four quartermasters, was made up of Chinese. The Pacific Mail Steamship Company had consistently argued that they needed a Chinese crew for economy reasons. The economy reasons were clearly brought out at a subsequent investigation which revealed the Chinese seamen were paid $9 a month, while union seamen got $40 a

month. An official of the company said it was necessary
or they would have to go out of business.

Many of the captains preferred Chinese crews, the
official added, because they obeyed orders better and
did their work better. It was a conclusion that was chal-
lenged quite strenuously at the official investigation.

As the *Rio* lay at anchor that afternoon a pilot boat
came alongside and Captain Fred W. Jordan clambered
aboard, carrying under his arm a very welcome bundle,
the late San Francisco newspapers. Captain Jordan had
some 28 years of experience in the Bay, the last 12 as a
pilot. He was known as "Lucky Jordan" because he had
never had a bad break in all his professional career, and
now he was about to pay for it.

Once aboard, Jordan was greeted warmly by the *Rio's*
skipper, Captain William Ward, a native of North Caro-
lina and at 38 years the youngest executive officer in
service of the company. He had entered the service of
Pacific Mail as a boy and worked his way from cadet
to captain. He had skippered a number of company ships
even at his young age and took command of the *Rio*
three years before.

The fog kept the *Rio* at anchor all night and shortly
after 4 a.m. the decision was made to proceed. Captain
Jordan, who survived, related what happened next:

"I had anchored the *Rio* off the Heads in 13 fathoms
of water for the night and there she lay until 4:30 a.m.
At that time we had the anchor up and got the *Rio* underway to come in. It was clear. There was a strong ebb
tide running. After we had been underway a few minutes
it became very thick because of a heavy tule fog."

Unknowingly, the *Rio* was being carried by a swirling
six knots ebb tide and slipped closer to the fog shrouded

Survivors of "Wreck of the Rio"

coast land. At 5:25 there was a grinding lurch that jarred the entire length of the 345-foot long ship with a sickening thud. The lights went out. The *Rio* had struck the Fort Point ledge and the bow rose high and the vessel listed sharply to port.

The Chinese crewmen in a babel of tongue ran to their posts and sleepy eyed passengers began to awaken. Captain Ward tied down the ship's whistle cord, sending a bellow of alarm. Then he ran down the corridors knocking and banging on doors to awaken passengers. His actions were credited with helping a number of the passengers escape. Two crewmen came running, saluted and asked for instructions.

"Lower the boats!" he shouted.

The crewmen saluted.

"Good bye, men. Be careful," the captain said.

It was the last seen or heard of Captain Ward, though he later became the subject of long and bitter debate through a variety of investigations as to whether he was at fault. The official conclusions were that he was. Strict company rules forbade bringing in a ship during fog.

On deck the passengers began milling about. Mrs. Wildman was waiting alongside a ready lifeboat. Pilot Jordan yelled at her to get into the boat. She refused, asking for her children. Consul Wildman came rushing up at that moment with the two children. Jordan took the boy to help. At that moment the vessel plunged and listed violently, throwing everyone into the water. Jordan continued his story.

"The boy had his arms around my neck as we went overboard and then under the water. The boy let go of my neck before we came up and I never saw him or his family again. They were all lost."

Jordan spotted a piece of floating wreckage and was pulled aboard by a Chinese crewman, who already had aboard a badly injured companion. They drifted for half an hour until Fisherman Fred Castarini came upon them. In his broken Genoese tongue Castarini related:

"I sail about and hear men yell. I look and see three men on some wreckage. I go and take them in my boat. One man pretty near dead. He spit blood and cannot stand up. Another man he nearly let go and drowned, but I pull him back. I take all back to Meiggs Wharf."

Antonio Venturini and Alberti Gibelli circled about picking up half drowned men and survivors clinging to bits of wreckage until they had 22 people aboard, 18 of them Chinese crewmen. They chugged their way quickly back to Meiggs Wharf.

Matteo de Jenaro and Santos Costa told this story:

"We headed our boat for the excitement and off in the distance we saw a great black mass going down, which we could make out was a steamer. We got close enough to see the masts disappear. Then we came to the lifeboat, which had 18 people, three of them women. The people in the boat were all shivering. We gave the women our oilskin coats, our vests and some heavy flannel shirts. They were all thankful. We took them home to the Wharf where there were lots of people."

One of those rescued in this lifeboat was Captain A. Hecht of the Imperial German Navy, who was on a world cruise.

Fisherman Andrew Adami told this story:

"When I first see the steamer I yell 'She's too close in shore!' As I yelled we came close enough to see a man on the bridge with a megaphone in his hand. 'Listen,' I say. Then we hear the voice, 'We're sinking, get help!'

Then the ship turned over and begin to sink. We look around, mama mia, we see people everywhere. Some have preservers. Some on rafts. I have been on bay many years but I never see anything like that. We start pulling them up one by one. Some people sink before we get there."

Adami and his crewmen picked up 11 people and was returning to Meiggs Wharf when he came upon an almost sinking raft, partly under water, with 10 wet and shivering Chinese crewmen aboard. They shouted pleas for help. Adami came by and tossed them a line and got safely to shore with all survivors. On land the Chinese clamored around Adami pounding him on the back in gratitude.

One of those rescued by Adami was Professor Wada. Roused from his sleep by the collision, he had hurriedly put on his clothes. Outside he met Dr. Onkawara and his wife. Together they ran through the social hall when they were struck square by a rush of water. Professor Wada was nearly rendered senseless and his companions were swept away and he never saw them again. Another wave swept Professor Wada through a hole in the side of the social hall and tossed him overboard. He was in the water for several minutes until he was pulled onto some wreckage by a Chinese crewman.

Russell Harper, who was rescued by Tony Silva, told his story:

"I was on deck trying to get to a boat when the steamer made a lunge forward. Water came along the deck, sweeping along with it. I felt something snap in my leg and the last thing I remember I was swept overboard. When I came to I was in the boat of an Italian fisherman who had taken me out of the water." Russell Harper suffered a broken right leg.

When news of the wreck was received, Meiggs Wharf became the point of concentration for the relief parties, and the landing point for survivors and bringing in of bodies. Relatives and friends came in hopes of learning something of those on board. Every time a fishing boat, or launch, headed for the Wharf the crowd surged forward. The landing of each body sent a chill through the crowd. The survivors were hurried to nearby shelter and given warm Italian prepared meals.

With the conclusion of the inquest and the inquiries into the sinking of the *Rio*, the attention of San Francisco and the rest of the country turned elsewhere. President McKinley was inaugurated and war was nearing between Russia and Japan. The Italian community met to commemorate the recent death of their beloved composer Giuseppe Verdi at Milan. The observances at the Tivoli Opera House was presided over by Mayor Phelan.

But the story of the *Rio* would not die. Slowly the legend began to form about this tragic vessel which has continued down through the years to this day.

First, the hulk of the *Rio* disappeared under somewhat puzzling circumstances. The first week of the wreck it was announced the hulk had been located offshore in 100 feet of water, and officials awaited calm weather to bring her up. But, when divers went down to locate her under the black waters of the bay they failed to find any signs of the wreck. To this day it has never been located.

In desperation the company finally offered $1,000 reward for anyone locating the hulk of the *Rio*. This offer brought many divers and salvage crews to the area, but even they failed. Although wreckage of the *Rio* littered the beach for months there was no clues as to the hulk itself. Over the decades maritime experts have advanced different theories of the missing *Rio*. It had been swept to sea, it had been carried into the inner bay and sucked into a bottomless pit, or it had settled into a cave beneath the Fort Point ledge.

If this were not enough to keep the legend of the *Rio* alive then reports of a kings ransom on board added to the intriguing mystery. News reports had it that $600,000 of gold bullion was aboard. Ship officials denied it, but the rumors were the company denied it to prevent treasure hunters from recovering the gold before it could be salvaged by the owners themselves. The reports gained credence when a New York insurance company confirmed another story, that 650 bales of highly valuable imported silk had been aboard, valued at $500 a bale, and the firm would pay half its value for any bales recovered. That only fed the flames and stimulated the imagination of seamen and landlubbers alike to keep alive the romantic myth.

Periodically salvage crews and divers announced expeditions to recover the gold, which grew in size over the years to one million, then two million and finally six million. For decades the story of the *Rio* crept into the headlines and Sunday supplements as new theories were advanced. One engineer even brought forth a sketch of a powerful electric magnet that he would use to recover the wreck. Whenever an unidentified piece of wreckage was found on the beach the legend of the *Rio's* treasure was revived.

Even the men of the Italian fishing fleet contributed their share to the legend. Being the ones who regularly travelled out past the scene of the wreck they often came back with stories of having sighted clues to the wreckage.

Though the legend of the *Rio* continues to grow, one story never changes. Out of the tragic wreck of the *Rio* was written the bravery of the Italian fishermen in their rescue efforts. Whenever the disaster was talked about the Italian fishermen came in for the highest praise.

It is unfortunate to report that this was not true in all quarters. Some reports ignored the role of the Italians in the rescue effort while other reports downgraded their role. It must be remembered for readers of today that the early 1900s was the beginning of the period of large immigration of Europeans to America, and with the immigrants coming there arose certain ethnic prejudices. The Chinese crewmen themselves were the subject of editorial comment the likes of which would shock present day readers.

No matter what the editorial comment, the Chinese appreciated the heroic work of the Italians in the rescue efforts. It was understandable why they should, for some 43 members of the Chinese crew were saved, practically all by the fishermen. The final toll showed 41 Chinese crewmen were lost and of the some 46 Asiatic passengers, only nine were saved.

In one of the little known gestures of the time the Chinese Six Companies, the ruling hierarchy of Chinatown, went among its members raising a cash fund which was distributed to the fishermen who had taken part in the rescue efforts. Nearly $200 each was distributed to each fishing boat.

Chapter 5

THE WAY IT WAS
AT OLD FISHERMAN'S WHARF

*B*efore it became fashionable at the turn of the century to drive to the Cliff House, or through Golden Gate Park, the old Fisherman's Wharf and North Beach was where San Francisco rolled up its shirt sleeves, opened its parasols and enjoyed a Sunday afternoon.

It was the thing to do to go to Meiggs' old lumber wharf, which ran from the North Beach shoreline some 1,600 feet into the bay. You rented a bathhouse and went in swimming there, or you promenaded along the Wharf with your girl friend on your arm. On the way back in from the end of the Wharf you might stop at Cockney White's museum and lose a quarter to the "educated pig" that played seven-up, the localized card game. If you were a gay blade with a hangover from Saturday night, you went to Driscoll's Salt Water Tub Bathing Emporium. You took your turn at a dip in the steaming sea water and then had a rubdown by Bathhouse Jack.

Perhaps you dropped in at Paddy Gleason's saloon, where Paddy often mixed the drinks with his right forefinger, the only finger he had on that hand. "It saves the trouble of keepin' me eye on the spoons," Paddy explained. After a snort or two, you might drop in across the street to Riley's Shooting Gallery or go to Mason's lot where for a small price you were enticed to try your luck at a greased pole with a $5 gold piece on top which was yours if you got there on your own. Few, if any, were so fortunate, but from a more practical point of view there was a ham a little lower on the pole and still lower to the ground was a silver dollar.

There was Zachariah Colby, who was crippled in the mines, and sold peanuts at the Wharf. Paddy Martin owned a pipe works near the Wharf, and it made a capital place for cockfights. Charles Walton, better known as "Charlie the Dumper," kept a junk shop at the Wharf. Charlie Schwartz's place was a popular crab spot, with mallets furnished free to crack the crab shells. Beer was five cents a glass and all the crab legs you could eat.

The first ferry terminal for a Sausalito ferry was also located at Meiggs Wharf, which helped change the spelling of the town's name. The town across the bay had always been known as "Saucelito," meaning "Grove of the Little Willows," but an errant sign painter made his mistake in foot high letters and the name change stuck.

The Merchants Exchange had a station at Meiggs Wharf, with two lookouts. They would get their signal from Telegraph Hill of an approaching ship, and go out in their boats to get the manifest from the ship's captain. Then back to Meiggs Wharf and the manifest of the ship's cargo was rushed down to Montgomery Street by a boy on horseback. The merchants would then bid for the merchandise even before the vessel had tied up at the docks.

This was also the ill-famed period along the Wharf area of shanghaiing, the nefarious business of supplying men for sea duty against their will. Beginning around 1850, it was perpetrated mostly on those who deserted their ships for the gold fields and returned with empty pockets. Then, after hundreds of vessels began pouring into San Francisco's bustling port, the victims were often sailors from other ships, and anyone else at loose ends around the waterfront. In 1878, for instance, it was estimated that 300 ships lay idle in the harbor, temporarily without crews.

The shanghaiing was done by such noted crimps with the unlikely names of Three Finger Curtin, Shanghai Brown, Hell-Cat Haggerty and Scabhouse Johnny. They usually delivered their human cargo unconscious from knockout drops, or bashed in heads. Most of those abducted did not revive until they were miles at sea. Frequently, too, they would discover they had signed away several months pay for clothing and other necessities never received.

Harassed skippers paid anywhere from $15 to $50 for each man delivered, the price depending on how much they needed a crew and what kind of ship they commanded. Sometimes the men were experienced sailors, but more often they were not.

But, the real place to go at the old Fisherman's Wharf was Abe Warner's famed "Cobweb Palace" for a dish of his wonderful clam, or crab chowder. As you sipped your chowder you marvelled at the festoons of cobwebs that hung from the gloomy rafters and the unique light fixtures and the cages in which was kept as exotic and crazy a menagerie that existed; a morose bear, a sleepy kangaroo and a family of sad-eyed monkees. The most popular attraction of all hung on a ring nailed to a rafter near the ceiling; a pet parrot who cackled the nonsensical line that made it almost as famous as its owner:

"I'll have a rum and gum! What'll you have?"

Presiding over this strange mixture of an attraction was friendly but eccentric Abe Warner who took his place in the long line of San Francisco's historical characters.

Old Timers at the Wharf

Abe was a native New Yorker who had been a Fulton Market butcher. In 1849, lured by the stories of gold, like everyone else, Abe followed the crowd to California. But alas, he soon discovered he was not the type to reap a fortune in the gold country and resumed his trade in a local meat stall. Then years after his arrival he bought a bar and restaurant at the shore end of Meiggs Wharf, at a point that is now Francisco Street and Powell. He continued to wear his butcher's frock coat and a silk top hat and a policy of unconcern for cleanliness on his part had the place looking, after a few months, as though for years it had been inhabited only by spiders and bats. Abe was superstitious about spiders and would never harm one. After a while, cobwebs covered the walls and ceilings and stretched in tenuous gray across the pictures on the wall.

On the back bar were such exotic items as sharks teeth and walrus tusks left with Warner by far-wandering sailors. The quality of Abe's chowders was unequivocal and the same held true of his imported French brandies and Spanish wines. He did not sell the plebeian whiskey. "Let 'em buy that in some low saloon," Abe said grumpily.

Once a week the floor was gone over and freshly dusted with white sand from the nearby beach. This was less a tribute to looks than a regard for the daily habits of the parrots and cockatoos that made the place their home.

There was a trap door in the sidewalk outside Abe's place through which would-be bathers descended to the water and swam out into the Bay. Down in the cellar there was a regular bathing establishment where swim suits could be rented and the swimmers clothing left in safety. Two horse cars ran regularly to Meiggs Wharf at the time. That is, they were supposed to run regularly, but the drivers killed time at the end of the run playing cards with Abe.

For some 34 years, Abe Warner ruled mightly and at times haughtily over this waterfront institution, until hard times came in 1893. The State had built a new sea wall on the waterfront, cutting off Meiggs Wharf from the bay. The old Alcatraz and Sausalito ferries no longer used Meiggs Wharf, and there were too many other places springing up to provide competition. The old Meiggs Wharf was dead, and the new and robust Fisherman's Wharf was ready and eager to spread its wings under the direction of the Italians.

Abe Warner's institution, like so many others, was sold under the auctioneers hammer, cobwebs, menagerie, and all. Warner, now a lonely old man with a white beard, moved to a cottage nearby.

Three years later he was found alone and dead in a Louis XIV bed, which he had managed to salvage from his bankruptcy. In a cage in his bedroom lay a pet cockatoo, which had preceded him in death by several days.

On the wall of the barren cottage there was hanging a lone portrait. Those who found the old man's body had to brush aside a thick skein of spider webs from the glass of the picture frame before they recognized the subject— it was a picture of Abe, taken when he was younger and smiling.

Oyster Pirates and Jack London

In the early 1870s, local fisheries tried the experiment of transplanting into San Francisco Bay some Eastern oysters. They proved popular and for the next 50 years in many of the shallow areas around San Francisco there were dozens of board fence enclosures dotting the skyline to signify locations of oyster beds.

In the days before the term "black market" became prominent, San Francisco and Fisherman's Wharf had their share of illegitimate traders called "Oyster Pirates." Of all the oyster pirates who sailed the Bay, the most famous was Jack London. At the age of 16, and on a borrowed $300, London bought the sloop *"Razzle Dazzle,"* and began the career in which his prowess eventually earned him the title "Prince of the Oyster Pirates." One of London's famed stories based on these experiences is "A Raid on the Oyster Pirates."

That the young writer London appreciated the Bay as a source of material is shown in the opening sequence of his classic story, "The Sea Wolf." This was the sinking of the ferry boat *"San Rafael"* off Fisherman's Wharf in November, 1901, a story that was later used in three different motion pictures.

This famed wreck took place because a dredge was anchored just west of Alcatraz Island while it was engaged in the removal of rock that was considered a menance to navigators. To avoid this dredge in the heavy fog of November 30, the ferry boat *"Sausalito"* followed a course east of Alcatraz. The skipper of the northbound *"San Rafael"* was steering around the island's east side as well, listening for warning whistles in the heavy fog.

He heard one, but too late. The *"Sausalito"* appeared ghostlike through the fog, and there was a quick, jarring impact and the sound of bending steel, splintering wood and breaking glass. The bow of the *"Sausalito"* plowed directly into the crowded restaurant of the *"San Rafael,"* killing a cook and two passengers. Alert crew members lashed the two ferries together and the rest of the passengers were able to climb to safety directly onto the *"Sausalito."* The lines were then severed and the *"San Rafael"* went to the bottom.

That London remained at liberty and lived to become something else proved him the exception among "oyster pirates." Most of them died young in waterfront brawls, or at the end of a prison rope, or were shot to death in gunfights with oyster bed watchmen.

The oyster beds which comprised their hunting grounds was along the ocean shores where operators grew large proportions of the oysters sold in San Francisco restaurants and bars of that era. They usually covered several square miles of muddy beach above which the water at high tide rose to about five feet. To protect the beds, oyster growers surrounded them with crude fences made of stakes and trimmed tree limbs driven into the mud. As a deterrent to raids, they ordered their watchmen to shoot trespassers.

Almost always the pirates worked in pairs. In their sloops they carried a rowboat, oyster rakes and many burlap sacks. Most of them picked calm, moonless nights for their work, reaching the oyster beds after dark. They preferred to anchor their sloops a fair distance from the beds and row to the flats, so that, if necessary, they could make a fast getaway.

Once at the beds they either chopped their way through the fence or slipped around the stakes until they found an opening. Then they rowed well into the bed, stripped and went overboard, wearing heavy leather gloves and boots to protect their hands and feet from the encrusted shells. In the darkness they worked rapidly with their rakes and and gloved hands and filled sack after sack with oysters. An hour's uninterrupted work usually yielded all that their rowboats could carry. If they were sighted by a watchman, it was either flight or fight. When it was fight, rifles cracked over the still water in a gun battle for their lives. If they got their haul back to the sloop undetected and unharmed, they would haul their sacks along the street, selling to individuals or to friendly and knowing restaurant owners.

The first introduction of a foreign oyster on a commercial basis was in 1868 when Mexican oysters were imported from Acapulco. The oysters were shipped by steamer and sold at the dock for 25 cents each and their gourmet appeal was so great that a notice was posted several days in advance of the steamers arrival. This business was not very profitable as many of the oysters spoiled during the trip. In 1870, when Eastern oysters began to be shipped to San Francisco on the newly completed continental railroad, the Mexican company went

out of business. Mexican oysters were again imported
during the period of 1897 to 1899 by Eli Gordon, but
conditions arising from the Spanish American War caused
him to discontinue the business.

In the early 1920 something happened to the Bay's
oysters. They began to have an unpleasant taste and
grew very slowly, or not at all. Apparently the waters
of the Bay were becoming too polluted with the wastes
of the harbors and the growing cities on its shores to continue to produce good oysters in commercial quantities.

Other places on the California coast, such as Tomales
and Drake's Bays, began to replace San Francisco Bay as
oyster producers. The beds and the plants here were
abandoned, although remains of them are still visible in
the shallow offshore areas. Most of the imported Eastern
oysters have died out but the small native variety still
grows in some quantities. Weekend oyster hunters wade
out around the rocks at low tide, at places like Coyote
Point, near San Mateo and McNear's Beach in Marin
to pry off the little animals for a palatable meal at home.

Chapter 6

WHALERS OFF FISHERMAN'S WHARF

*M*any landlubbers dining in the comfortable warmth of Fisherman's Wharf restaurants are surprised to learn that among the many craft which pass within sight on the waters of the Bay are modern whaleboats. If nothing else, it is a reminder of one of the most fabled aspects of California's fishing history, that during the Gold Rush the town of San Francisco was headquarters for whaling ships of the Pacific and for a time in the 1880s became the greatest whaling port in the world.

During this period of San Francisco whaling glory, it has been estimated that a thousand whales passed daily in the waters where Fisherman's Wharf diners now gaze. San Francisco's role began dwindling in 1884 when the number passing by shrank to less than 40 and by 1895 the profitable whaling industry was at an end. Three of San Francisco's whalers closed their career at sea in 1865 at the point of a gun. They were the victims of the cannon of the Confederate raider *"Shenandoah."*

These facts are often astonishing to many visitors at Fisherman's Wharf. They are more familiar with the story of the New Bedford whalers, who with their neighbors from Nantucket, New London and Fairhaven, turned the Pacific into a vast American whale fishery. However, numerous gray whales frequented the shallow waters and lagoons off the California coast and were easily sighted and captured, and towed ashore for processing. Some 16 whaling stations were located along the coast, and almost all marketed their products in San Francisco.

Whaling came to San Francisco because of the Gold Rush. When news of the gold strike reached the Eastern cities the adventurers and dreamers who headed for San Francisco found that the best means of transportation were the hardy whaling vessels that were used to making their way around the horn. Enterprising whaling ship owners lined their pockets by booking passage to the gold fields, while other gold hunters signed on as deckhands and then conveniently jumped ship when it docked. With these whaling ships in San Francisco harbor, what better use than to do the business they were built for, capturing whales. The whaling industry grew in leaps and bounds when discouraged sailors came back from the gold fields, broke and hungry. They signed up again on the whalers and this time meant business, for they wanted anything to get away from the land that had promised them so much and delivered them so little.

Prior to this period whalers had come into San Francisco Bay, as early as 1820, only to load up with fresh water and supplies and to cut firewood at nearby Angel Island. Richard Dana described one such visit to San Francisco in "Two Years Before the Mast."

The Mexican government, which ran things then, began taking alarm at the number of gringo whaling ships coming into the Bay in the early 1800s, and fearing the Americans would get a foothold in California, imposed restrictions against the whalers. This caused the whalers to move their supply rendezvous to Hawaii, then known as the Sandwich Islands, which they used until 1865, when they again returned to using San Francisco Bay. The Hawaiian government forced the issue by not allowing whaling vessels to carry a native away from the islands without posting a bond of $600 for his return.

An Early Fish Counter at the Wharf

The whalers, and the whales, have left their mark in San Francisco legend and history. California author Evelyn Wells wrote a book-length story of whaling in the Bay in the San Francisco *Call and Post* in November, 1920.

The San Francisco newspapers had a field day in February, 1938, when a 100-ton, 65 foot whale, given the name of Mopey Dick, was spotted in the Bay, and for three days the editorial and maritime search continued, giving rise to stories of the glorious days of whaling that used to be.

Newsman Baron Muller was pictured on the front page of the *News* in the costume of Captain Ahab, along with a beauty queen of the day on his lap. "There is no reason for Captain Muller, alias Ahab, to put out to sea to search for a whale," the paper reported, "but whaling has been in his blood since he learned how to harpoon at a fraternity house dining table at Stanford University."

The hunt, by then reported in the press around the world, came to an end when the whale was washed ashore dead, and Captain Muller wanted to know if whales are washed ashore and then die, or die and then are washed ashore. In a few days the problem of the expired whale became evident to all in the area. Joseph Alioto, president of the International Fish Company at Fisherman's Wharf, came to the rescue and offered to remove the whale. Alioto, whose namesake son grew up to be mayor of San Francisco, barged it past his colleagues at Fisherman's Wharf to a plant at Islais Creek, where portions of the carcass were melted down into oil and tallow and other parts converted into fertilizer and chicken feed. The teeth of the whale were turned over to authorities for exhibit at the San Francisco's World's Fair that opened the following year.

Old timers recalled that two years before a display of deep sea life, which included a 68-ton whale, had been exhibited from a railroad car parked on the tracks near Fisherman's Wharf. Still other old timers, and newspaper writers, reminisced about another whale legend in San Francisco. It put San Francisco in the same league with those wonderful old prints that showed a raging old whale, covered with barnacles, smashing a whaleboat in two with a single blow of its mighty flukes. Two generations of movie goers saw John Barrymore, and then Gregory Peck, stump about the deck of the *Pequod* in "Moby Dick" in their mad and fatal pursuit of the great white whale without knowing of San Francisco's legend. Readers will be interested to know that such an event was reported in 15 fathoms of water six miles southeast of the Farallone Islands in the evening of July 21, 1900, in which a large boat was attacked and sunk by a monster whale.

It was the pilot boat *Bonita,* an 81-foot schooner of 75 tons, launched only eight years before at a cost of $22,000, and the pride of the Bar Pilots fleet. Her trim lines, her gleaming brass and her handsome decks gave her a saucy air and drew waterfront loungers to her pier to watch her arrival whenever they saw her heading for home.

On July 21, the *Bonita* tacked her way through the Heads on a routine assignment with five pilots aboard. She was taking Captain E. M. Freeman to a German bark and then was to cruise outside the harbor to meet any other arriving ships that would require the services of other bar pilots. On their way they spied a school of whales, blowing and rolling and sounding with great upward swings of their giant flukes.

At 9:30 that evening the *Bonita* having transferred pilot Freeman to the German bark, was lying on a calm sea, with all sails set and riding the swells. Two of the captains had retired to the bunks below. Suddenly something struck the *Bonita* a staggering blow on the port quarter. Like a toy ship the *Bonita* raised from the water and heeled wildly to the starboard. All on board were knocked sprawling by the impact.

"Get into your clothes, boys," yelled one of the pilots. "That's a whale that hit us for sure."

Staggering to their feet the men glanced at the sea to see what caused the crash. They later reported that there, so close to the *Bonita's* hull that they might have leaped on its back, and fully as long as the ship itself, was a giant whale.

"I saw the whale when I rushed on deck," said another pilot. "The whale was stunned, but he recovered himself quickly and if he would have come back for more I don't know where we would have landed."

In the midst of this confusion a humorous incident was recorded. Of the two pilots below, one weighed nearly 300 pounds and was short and bay windowed, and the second was slight of build. They had rushed on deck hastily tugging at their trousers and shoes, only to discover they had switched clothes. "At the sight of them we doubled up amidships with laughter," one of the crew reported.

Soon the sea was pouring into the ship from both bow and stern. Hastily gathering clothing, compasses and personal effects the crew took to the *Bonita's* two lifeboats. A few hours later the *Bonita* went to the bottom. The men rowed for five hours before being picked up by the *Gracie S,* a sister pilot boat. In one of the interesting aftermaths, one of the pilots shortly afterwards was put aboard the incoming steamer *Wellington* to pilot her into port, as he apparently had not been too shaken by the experience to continue his exacting job.

Down through the years the legend of the sinking of the *Bonita* by a whale, or by something, has been questioned on occasions by salty mariners, though it has been officially reported and described in numerous articles and books without question. Al Harman, the doughty veteran librarian and historian at San Francisco's Maritime Museum, was one of those who asked questions. This created the need for historical research.

Several days after the wreck in 1900, a waterfront writer for the *Chronicle* mentioned briefly at the end of his column that none of the incoming ships had reported seeing any wreckage from the pilot boat, though he noted skippers did report seeing whales. He also wrote that prior to the *Bonita* a number of stories had circulated about vessels being struck by whales outside the Farallones, but none were accepted by seafaring men.

The best investigators of the legend would have been waterfront reporters of the time, but newspapers in July of 1900 had other important matters concerning them. Screaming headlines for weeks told details of the Boxer Rebellion, when American troops were sent to help crush the Chinese revolt of a military group called I Ho Ch'uan, otherwise known as the Boxers. It was the days of the "Yellow Peril" and atrocity stories from China did not leave much room for local news.

William Jennings Bryan became the Democratic Party nominee the same month at Kansas City, and earlier in the month 350 people died and 500 were injured when fire swept through three ocean liners at piers of the North German Lloyd Lines at Hoboken, New Jersey. So, the story of the *Bonita* gathered dust in the files.

Perhaps the only challenge to the legend, facetious as the challenge might have been, was a pleasant little doggerel writen by Newsman Will Irwin shortly after the wreck. This is the same Irwin who later went to New York from where he wrote in 1906, after San Francisco's earthquake and fire, his famous story, "The City That Was." This is what Irwin had to say about the *Bonita:*

Oh, tell me, tell me, sailormen
　　Oh, tell me pilots four.
How come your boat is in Davy's locker
　　And yourselves on the balmy shore.

We're blunt and rough, says the pilots
　　And we tell no fancy yarn.
So, here's our tale in outline form
　　Though it smelleth of fish, by darn.

We struck no rock and we struck no shoal
      As we passed the Farallones.
But we struck a whale who flipped his tail
      And sent us to Davy Jones.

And this we'll add, said the pilots sad
      We've sailed near the arctic snows.
And we've felt the breeze of the tropic seas
      Where the dreadful typhoon blows.

But never yet has pilots met
      A critter in all the zones.
Like the sarsy whale with the iron clad tail
      Who lives near the Farallones.

Chapter 7

THE CHINESE AT
FISHERMAN'S WHARF

*M*unicipal Judge Harry Low of San Francisco, a brilliant graduate of the University of California at Berkeley and the first man of Chinese ancestry appointed to the bench in San Francisco, was speaking at a retirement dinner for a popular policeman. As he looked around the crowded dining room, filled to overflowing with a typical San Francisco cosmopolitan flavor, Judge Low remarked:

"I am glad to see so many native Irishmen here, who helped us build the railroad, and so many Italians who helped us start Fisherman's Wharf!"

As the laughter died down the realization came that the role of the Chinese in building Fisherman's Wharf is not as widely known as their role in building the railroads of California. The sight of high-prowed Chinese sailing junks in San Francisco Bay coming to dock at Fisherman's Wharf today would be a curiousity attracting a great crowd. It was not an unusual sight before the turn of the century.

The Chinese, and the Italians, have a distinguished history in making the San Francisco Bay shrimp, technically named Crago Franciscorum, into the City's pride and joy. The Bay shrimp are unique and succulent and have contributed to the gourmet's delight for more than a century.

Before the Civil War, individual Italian fishermen were dragging their hand nets through the shallows of Hunters Point and bringing up shrimp. The Chinese took over some ten years later.

The Italian shrimp nets were 60 feet long and kept open by long poles cut from Eucalyptus saplings. Weights along the bottom scuffed up the soft ooze where the shrimps flourished. It was customary to drag for about an hour and then haul in the nets, sometimes producing a catch of 100 pounds or more in a single drag. They usually fished at high tide, when there was a maximum of motion in the water. The nets were played out at about two miles an hour, then hauled in. They poured the contents on the deck and sorted out the live fish, which were tossed back into the water. With a wooden scoop, the fishermen would shovel the live, squirming shrimp into great baskets which held from 100 to 125 pounds of shrimp each. While making the second drag, the fishermen would keep the shrimp in the basket fresh by pouring sea water over them.

The Chinese entered the commercial shrimp market in 1871 and by 1875 it was estimated there were 1,500 Chinese engaged in catching and drying shrimp in the Bay Area. The Chinese entered the shrimp market in San Francisco for a very simple and logical reason; they had no other place to go. You must recall that this was a sad period of anti-Chinese sentiment in California and the nabobs of railroad fame, in 1865, were importing great numbers of Chinese to work on the railroads. As their work finished on the railroad they drifted into San Francisco and sought refuge in the familiar sights and sounds of the established Chinatown area. Had they been left alone it would have been one matter, but along in 1870 an instigator and voluble orator of his time named Denis Kearney was going up and down the streets of

San Francisco preaching the gospel that "the Chinese must go!"

With the persecution of the Chinese so rampant, some 3,000 of them fled to the isolated Marin Cove which now bears their name, China Cove. Their rickety shanties were built on stilts similar to the shacks along the Yangtze River. The slopes hugging the shoreline in back of their homes were terraced with gardens of long string beans and heads of Chinese cabbage.

How the Chinese entered the shrimp business is the source of an interesting story. According to the legend, which sounds quite a bit fishy, a Chinese cook begged a handful of shrimp from an Italian fisherman at Hunters Point. He cooked them in a handy tin can and was so delighted with the flavor that he told his tong chief. The sagacious tong chief, knowing a good thing when he tasted it, immediately sent to China for a supply of nets and a few experienced fishermen.

Be that as it may, by 1897 there were 26 known Chinese shrimp camps in the area, but by 1910 this had been reduced to 19. Of these, three were located in the cove just north of South San Francisco, five at Hunters Point, four near Red Rock and the others near Point San Pedro in Marin County.

The Chinese acquired a lease to their fishing grounds from the Chinese companies, located with offices in China-town, a practice quite contrary to our law but in accordance with a more binding Chinese precedent. The lessees maintained the boats, gear and building, and operated on a "share the profit" basis among themselves. Each camp had its own sailing junk, living quarters for the several boat crews, sheds for cooking and grading the catch, wooden platforms for sun drying, net tanning vats, dry racks for nets and gear storage sheds. Each had a rickety dock where boats tied up and unloaded.

Each shrimp camp had its "Joss House," where much incense was burned. The fisherman's "joss," or idol, was consulted many times throughout the season. In the little known ways of the Chinese, each shrimper paid $2.50 a month to worship at the "Joss House." In an interesting comparison of values, English instruction was offered there at $2 a month.

During the time they were coming to Fisherman's Wharf, the Chinese lent a most colorful and exotic addition as their Chinese junks were fashioned after those of their native land. Usually the captain squatted on the afterdeck with a piece of red flannel around his head. Members of the crew wore the regulation Chinese bamboo hat shaped like an inverted basket. The trawling junks, with an eye painted on each side of the prow, participated in festive Dragon boat races held every year. When asked why the eye was there, the Chinese would reply: "No eyes, no see where boat going!"

The Chinese used a centuries old oriental method of set-net fishing called the shrimp net, a tide operated type of gear traditionally used in China. These nets were staked to the mud bottom in a line and changed with the flow of each tide. They were both ingenious and efficient, and much more practical than those used by the Italians.

The catch of shrimp were taken to shore in deep round baskets, imported from China, where they were immediately cooked.

The shrimp were plopped into vats of boiling water where they cooked for nearly 10 minutes. The water was seasoned with rock salt to prevent the shrimp from getting too soft. The cooked shrimp was then dried in the sun for several days on low wooden platforms, and the heavy aromas became a natural beacon for passing boats. Regularly, a hoe-like broom was delicately used to spread the layers of shrimp without bruising them.

When they were exposed to the sun for four or five days they were sufficiently dried. They were then crushed under large wooden pestles. More often they were trod upon by women and children wearing especially made wooden shoes. This crushing method was for the purpose of loosening the meat from the outer chitinous covering. The shrimp were then taken up and placed in baskets which were violently shaken until the meat was removed from the shells.

Another method used was to remove the shells by placing the dried shrimp in a winnowing machine, a rather crude affair constructed by the Chinese on precisely the same principle as used for winnowing grain. The meat and shells were then packed for exportation, the shells being utilized in China as a fertilizer.

As for the local market, the Chinese shrimp were sold for 8 to 14 cents a pound. Because of the nature of the times, including an atmosphere of anti-Chinese legislation, it was required that a Caucasian captain make delivery of the shrimp to Fisherman's Wharf. Much of this explains why the bulk of the shrimp was dried and exported to China.

For the local market, it was the custom of a number of San Francisco restaurants to place a heaping plate of cooked shrimp before the patron so that he could nibble while looking over the menu.

Another fishing almost wholly confined to the Chinese at that time was the collection of abalone shells. They dried and slit the meats, which was highly prized in China. The shells were polished and then used for ornaments, and even jewelry.

When the Chinese used gill nets, their mode of fishing proved very peculiar to the Occidental. Once having set these nets the Chinese crew members remained close by in their boats to watch the approaching schools of fish. If they did see the fish close to the net, but not disposed to enter, they set up a terrific babel of shouting, pounding the side of the boat with clubs and splashing oars in the water to frighten the fish so that they would in their wild rush to escape swim into the meshes of the net.

But, sentiment and the prejudice of the times turned against the Chinese. In 1901, the State Legislature imposed a closed season during the months of May through August. The Chinese fought this law through to the United States Supreme Court, without success. In 1905, they were successful in getting the ban repealed, but they were further curtailed in 1909. In 1911, the use of the shrimp net was prohibited. Hunters Point was ultimately taken over by the Navy, which further reduced their number. This unpopular reaction, and more up-to-date methods of fishing and processing caused the gradual abandonment of shrimping by the Chinese.

There was another factor that reduced the number of Chinese shrimp fishermen. The destruction of some small fish in the shrimp nets opened an opportunity for unscrupulous politicians to propose hampering legislation so that a campaign fund to kill the bill would be collected from the Chinese. The fishermen knew they were being cheated, but they paid rather than fight. After all, such methods had been familiar to their ancestors for centuries.

Chapter 8

THE WHARF AND WORLD WAR II

$\mathcal{T}$he war came to Fisherman's Wharf in January of 1942.

Benito Mussolini was strutting noisily across the map of Europe with his friend Hitler, America was reacting from the shock of Pearl Harbor, and public officials were daily voicing warnings of impending attacks over the waters of the Golden Gate and that San Francisco would be bombed at any moment. Rumors of enemy subs off the Gate and reported landings of saboteurs were many. San Francisco's two Italian language newspapers, *Il Corriere del Popolo* (liberal) and *L'Italia* (conservative) were at war over who in San Francisco had, or had not, been favorable to the Fascist cause.

Tempers grew short at the Wharf, and in North Beach, as the war reached into every facet of life. It was not to be a very pleasant part of San Francisco history, or America's either for that matter.

While the sons of many Italian families were going to war, Congressmen demanded the Government take full and immediate action to clear all strategic areas of enemy aliens. Accordingly, on January 30, Attorney General Francis Biddle issued a sweeping and far reaching order that all enemy aliens be removed from the waterfront district. Italy was then at war with the United

States. The order was unequivocal in naming Fisherman's Wharf as one of the spots to be closed.

"No enemy alien will be permitted to live in a forbidden zone, to work there or even visit there," the order read. "The exclusion of aliens from the prohibited areas not only will aid the national defense but will also protect the alien himself." The order included German and Japanese nationals. The Japanese in San Francisco, and throughout the west, were later sent off to relocation camps and their property confiscated.

Governor Culbert Olson of California went further, saying he would ask for authority to revoke all business and professional licenses, including alien food handlers. "If the State government is licensing aliens to do business," said Governor Olson, "then we're contributing to the possibility of fifth column activity."

Then Governor Olson struck closer to the heart of Fisherman's Wharf activity. "It is my feeling that there is no place in California for private foreign language schools operated or financed by the nationals of foreign powers, whether in peace time or in time of war," he was quoted as saying.

The Americanization classes that had been sponsored for the last 11 years by the Crab Fishermen's Association had to close down. A disturbing fact was disclosed when it was revealed that only 75 of the 250 members of the Association were citizens, though many of them had been in San Francisco for years. It was further estimated that some 1,400 Italians from the 2,000 employed in the fishing industry would be affected by the order.

What had delayed so many of the Italians from becoming citizens? Paul Aglietti, business manager of the Crab Fishermen's Association, gave part of the answer.

"Many of the members and their wives have been here for 20 years and more," he said. "They have raised families, trained their sons to be fishermen and have bought homes. It is hard for them. There are so many dialects they must first be taught pure Italian, then taught to change that into English."

What did the fishermen have to say? What of those patriarchs of Fisherman's Wharf, those sun-tanned, weather-beaten fishermen who were now being banished from the haunts they had known for two score years? What of their fishing boats that would now stand idle under the grim eyes of armed sentries?

There was Lorenzo Manisalco, stocky, barrel-chested with a granitic, weather-hewn face, who came from Sicily as a young man and became the father of 12 children, four of whom were even then serving in the armed forces. Lorenzo, the "King of the Crab Fishermen," who was universally regarded as the bravest man at the Wharf, a legend in his time. Lorenzo was not a citizen.

"I try, try, try to become a citizen," Lorenzo explained. He knocked his head with his closed fist. "My head, she too damm hard. Can't learn. Can't write. Go to school and get first papers. Gomback to get second papers. Still can't write. Can't get citizen. What I do now, monkey around? Can't get job, not a citizen. I know nothing but fish. I can fish as good as anybody."

There was Camillo Borruso, another veteran of the sea.

"Why didn't I go to school sooner?" he groaned. "I musta been nuts." He spread his hands in a futile gesture. "I worked-a hard, seven kids, I had to support. My son, Giuseppe, he is 22, and in the Navy. I buy— we all buy—bonds, because we love this country. I am a loyal American."

Giuseppe DiMaggio, then 69, and the father of baseball stars Joe DiMaggio, and Dom, Vince and Tom, who even then owned a modern Wharf restaurant in the shadows where he had toiled as a fisherman. Then retired, he enjoyed hanging around the Wharf and his son's restaurant, swapping stories of the old days and listening with swelling pride as visiting tourists talked of Joe and Dom hitting home runs. The elder DiMaggio had come to the United States in 1905 but he was not a citizen, and an alien under the law.

"I guess I can't hang around any more," he lamented.

Antone Sabella, a citizen by virtue of being American born and now the owner of one of the better known restaurants at the Wharf serving a select clientele, had tears in his eyes as he talked of "Papa." Papa was Luciano Sabella, then 71, who had been fishing at Fisherman's Wharf for more than 50 years.

"He is a good American," said Sabella. "This is a good government. They will help. We all have hope and faith in America."

Sabella's faith, like those of the other Italians was a justified one. Many prominent Italians worked long and quietly behind the scenes. They were successful. Less than a year later, on November 5, 1942, Secretary of the Navy Frank Knox lifted the alien restrictions so that the Italians could return to their fishing boats at Fisherman's Wharf. He changed the status of Italian nationals from "enemy alien" to plain "alien." The change in status enabled an estimated 300 fishermen to immediately go to sea again, and others quickly followed. With the new status, were some new rules. Every fisherman who went to sea was to have an identification card from the Captain of the Port. Either the captain of the crew of a vessel, or 50 per cent of the crew, had to be an American citizen.

Little did the fishermen care. They were going back to sea, adding but a small historical link to those memorable lines:

"A fisherman, taking his living from the sea, is a timeless figure that survives the rise, decline and falls of kings and governments."

On another local front, a committee of prominent Italians organized to meet with General John L. DeWitt, the Chief of the Western Defense Command who had ordered the evacuation of all people of Japanese ancestry in California, and with then Attorney General Earl Warren.

Heading the committee was Chauncey Tramutolo, who was later to become United States Attorney for the district. Others were Dr. Charles Ertola, then a State Agricultural Commissioner and later a prominent Supervisor; Attorneys Elios P. Anderlini and Tobias J. Bricca; Walter Carpeneti, later to become a highly respected judge; John B. Molinari, who rose to become presiding Justice of the State Appellate Court, and Armond De-Martini, publisher of the *Little City News*.

"Warren was receptive, cordial and understanding," Justice Molinari reported in a statement published some 20 years later. "He assured us of his confidence in the loyalty of those of Italian ancestry in the United States.

"We were unable to meet with General DeWitt personally, but did meet with one of his ranking staff officers. He was cordial and listened patiently to what we had to say.

"I have a vivid memory of Chauncey Tramutolo's fine and persuasive presentation. Particularly impressive, was the manner in which lawyer Tramutolo pleaded the case of those of Italian ancestry both in and out of uniform."

Needless to say, wrote Molinari, the feared evacuation of Italians in San Francisco did not come to pass. Was it the committee's efforts which caused General De-Witt's discretion to be exercised against the exclusion of Italians?

History need not seek the answer. The results speak for themselves.

Chapter 9

MEN WHO GO DOWN TO SEA

$\mathcal{S}$an Francisco owes much of her tradition to those hardy breed of men who go down to the sea from Fisherman's Wharf. These crab fishermen are the most intrepid mariners afloat, and a happy lot. They go into the wide spaces of the Pacific Ocean in their tiny boats with a respectful prayer for the saints, but not too much respect for charts, buoys and channels. To these men of the sea, fishing is not the hazard it appears to others. It is an adventure. The wind, tide and the weather make life for the fisherman unpredictable, and sometimes dangerous, but it is still an adventure.

There are legends of great fishermen at Fisherman's Wharf like Tony Scafani, John Napoli and perhaps the greatest legend of all—Lorenzo Manisalco, the "King of Crab Fishermen." Universally regarded as the bravest man on the Wharf, he carried a watch fob presented to him by his fellow fishermen inscribed: "Al Campione"— "To the Champion." For nearly half a century he consistently returned to the Wharf with the biggest catch in the fleet. Legend had it that he could bring in as much as any two men on the Wharf. As the legend grew, the number grew to four and finally one historian unblinkingly wrote that Manisalco could bring in as much as five men.

But the Campione was indeed a brave one. He piloted his white *"San Cristoforo"* out into the Gate in weather that kept most other craft moored to the dock.

Sometimes his was the only boat out the Gate. He set his ring nets along the beach nearer the line of breakers than any other fisherman dared to venture.

"Every day," recalled an old timer at the Wharf Association, "Someone would call up very excited and say 'There's a white boat in the surf near the beach.' I would say relax, it's only Manisalco. 'Is he crazy?' they would ask. No, I would say, it's only Manisalco."

Such daring exacts its toll. Twice mountainous breakers smashed Manisalco's boat and rolled it over. The second time another fisherman came to his rescue, but he refused to get aboard the rescue craft until its skipper would put out a line on the *"San Cristoforo"* and tow it in. The rescuer, fearing for the safety of his own boat in the breakers, declined to do so. The two fishermen shouted Italian imprecations at each other over the roar of the surf until Manisalco turned numb in the icy waters and almost lost his hold, then was dragged into the rescue boat, still protesting. The *'San Cristoforo"* was smashed in the breakers. But the Campione bought a new *"San Cristoforo"* from his earnings and soon was hauling up crabs again barely outside the line of breakers.

Old timers recall Tony Scafani, a wiry, white-haired fisherman with 45 years of fishing experience. They remember the day when Tony crossed the bar on calm seas in his 26-footer and started south. Two hours later he was in a full gale and couldn't get back. The Coast Guard couldn't locate his boat in the welter of angry waters for two days and gloom spread over Fisherman's Wharf. For those two days and nights Tony worked pumping and praying continuously as he rode the mountainous waves. At last, exhausted, he beat his way around Point Lobos and up to the Gate and finally welcome land.

But, there's always the need to go back. Once Tony made a 40-mile round trip to his trap lines in a fog that

Mending the Nets at the Wharf

(Convention Bureau Photo)

tied up other ships. He needed the money. The Wharf
was completely blotted out when he left, so he counted
20 minutes to get down to the Gate, and cruised straight
to the sea for an hour. Finally, ahead in the murky darkness, he heard the foghorn on the lightship. He was 14
miles off shore in the shipping lanes. Cutting behind the
lightship, he ran 20 minutes to the northwest and inter-
cepted his trap lines. He collected his crabs, backtracked
to the lightship and groped his way through the symphony

of fog horns at the Gate. Fifteen minutes after he docked, and sold his catch to the wholesalers, the sun came out over San Francisco.

Perhaps the most famous story of all on Fisherman's Wharf, a true story in all its detail, is that of Fisherman John Napoli. The story began at 4:50 p.m. on a heavily fog bound afternoon in August of 1950 and the 15,000 ton hospital ship *USS Benevolence*, heavily loaded with 526 people aboard, including two crews, was completing a long series of tests outside the Golden Gate. On its return, in the heavy fog, it collided with the freighter *Mary Luckenbach*, ripping a 50-foot hole in the *Benevolence*, above and below the water line. The *Benevolence* began to list sharply. Within five minutes the main deck was awash and the vessel continued to roll. People began to go over the side as the ship finally sank.

Fisherman John Napoli had been trolling off the Farallones all day in his 34-foot boat, the *"Flora."* He had a good catch, 500 pounds of gleaming silver salmon lying in four big boxes on the deck. He was on his way back to Fisherman's Wharf, still several miles offshore, when he noticed what appeared to be a large turtle in the water. A few minutes later he spotted the freighter *Mary Luckenback* and a Coast Guard boat approached and someone shouted at him. He thought it was something about a man overboard. He recalled what he had seen and he waved for the Coast Guard boat to follow him as he swung the *"Flora"* around to the spot where he had seen the "turtle." It was a man, bleeding from cuts and nearly unconscious. Napoli hauled him aboard. As he swung around the fog lifted momentarily and Napoli saw all around him the horror at the scene of the wreck.

'God Almighty," he said afterwards. "Those heads bobbin' all around like seagulls sitti' on the water. My hair stand up."

Time was short, but Napoli's instincts went to work. He dragged more survivors over the rail of his boat. Most of them were blue and shivering, hardly able to speak or pull themselves aboard.

"I have to make plenty room so they don't hurt the other guys when they flop down," said Napoli, "So I throw the boxes of fish overboard."

When the boat was full he took his human catch to the *Mary Luckenback*. As the helpless survivors were transferred to the big ship in wire baskets, the *"Flora"* rose and fell on the swells and banged against the steel hull of the freighter until her rail buckled.

Then Napoli set out for more. Occasionally the fog lifted and he could see other craft of the rescue fleet— Coast Guard cutters, private yachts and other fishing boats who had rushed to the calls for help—a miniature Dunkirk armada.

"The noise was something terrible," Napoli said later. "When I get to thinking about it in my sleep it makes me jump outta bed. You hear 500 people in the water hollerin', you never get it outta your system."

Napoli fished one of the hospital ship nurses over the side. Then another and another. He found 16 Navy men all hanging together.

"I get them to the boat, but I just ain't got the strength left to pull 'em up," said Napoli. "I stood there and cried. I couldn't help it. I bawl like a baby."

Finally, he tied the swimmers to the crumpled rail of the *"Flora"* and towed them to another boat where they were picked up.

Owing to the remarkable work of the Coast Guard and the rescue craft, 498 of the 526 people aboard the

Benevolence were saved. The death toll made it one of the Bay's worst disasters in history. Altogether, Napoli had pulled 54 people from the water.

As a result of exposure and the strain of pulling survivors aboard the *"Flora,"* Napoli was hospitalized. Owing to consequent spinal trouble he was unable to continue fishing and had to put up the *"Flora"* for sale. Reporter John Campbell Bruce learned of Napoli's plight and wrote of his misfortunes in a national magazine. Sympathetic readers donated more than $1,000 and the Secretary of the Navy sent a check for $4,000.

Unfortunately, the gifts and the compensation could not make up for the loss of his livelihood due to the injuries he incurred. Deprived of his trade as a fisherman, he was able to eke out a living by taking whatever work he could find on the docks. When Napoli was hospitalized, he recalled that many of the people he rescued, including the nurses and the 16 Navy men, came to see him in the hospital and some offered him money. The fisherman recalled that he shrugged off the gifts from them.

"You save a fella's life," said Napoli in the tradition of Fisherman's Wharf and the sea, "you don't take money for it. They someday do the same for you."

But, he paid a high price for his heroism. John Napoli, to whom the sea was a way of life, would never fish again. His back was ruined. Napoli sold the *"Flora"* at a loss, and he sold his crabtraps. Painfully he began a new adjustment to a life ashore. It was hard and in the next ten years medical bills piled up and in 1958 his wife died.

In 1961, Congress voted him $25,000 in compensation and Napoli beamed: "I square up with everybody now." In time his exploits were forgotten and he died quietly in 1969 in a Terra Linda, Calif., hospital.

Chapter 10

DAMNDEST FINEST FOG
IN THE WORLD

*T*here is nothing on earth exactly like the fog of San Francisco Bay.

If you are sitting in one of the wonderful view restaurants at Fisherman's Wharf, or just plain visiting San Francisco, and you gaze out onto the magnificent view of the Golden Gate during the spring and summer months, you will see a wispy finger of vapor entering the Bay beneath the 230-foot high deck of the Golden Gate Bridge. In the course of a few hours it will thicken until it is a solid mass moving through the mile-wide straight into the Bay.

This is San Francisco's famed fog and automatic air conditioner—the damndest finest fog in the world as far as provincial residents are concerned. While it sometimes chills the bones of thinly-clad summer tourists, San Franciscans love the fog because it keeps the city cool during the summer. Since temperatures in Golden Gate country rarely rise above 75 degrees, or dip below 45, San Franciscans are temperamentally and constitutionally unacclimated to hot weather.

When the mercury hits 80, the natives begin to wilt. If it stays there, they get mad. As a rule, two or three warm days are all it takes to turn on the fog and cool things off.

San Francisco's famed fog finds its most dramatic access at the slot where the Pacific penetrates the continental well—the Golden Gate, and gives the natives of Fisherman's Wharf a ringside seat to one of the most spectacular sights in the world when the fog begins to enter the Bay.

San Francisco fog differs from other fogs, which is normally caused by a thin strata of warm moist air over cold water surfaces. In most parts of the world, fog traditionally is a dark, disagreeable smudge that hides the sun, obscures the vision and casts a damp spell over the land. In San Francisco, the fog is a thing of beauty and wonder that is fantastic in shape and motion.

San Francisco's fog is caused by a rare combination of water, winds and topography. It is formed by the mixture of two air streams, one warm and the other not so warm, but heavily laden with water vapor.

The streak of cold water along the coast is a basic part of San Francisco's summertime air conditioning system. The wind from the west, having traversed thousands of miles of ocean, absorbs great quantities of moisture from the surface by evaporation. When it approaches the coast, the air comes in contact with the cold, upwelled waters and causes its moisture to condense.

The same process that causes moisture to form on the outside of a glass of cold water takes place here on a mammoth scale. Rather than clinging to the outside of the glass, the drops of water condensed in the sea breeze cling to the minute particles of salt that have been thrown into the air with the spray.

Thus, as the wind blows over the cold surface, the drops of water continue to form until they create a haze, which soon thickens into fog. It may range in width from

100 yards to more than 100 miles along much of California's coast.

The long, rolling, shifting gray bank moves silently into the Golden Gate at a rate of 10 to 20 miles an hour, carried inward by the moving air. At the maximum, perhaps a million gallons of water an hour float through the Gate as vapor. The fog formed in this way is literally a cloud resting on the water. It may later rise into the air and look more like the conventional idea of a cloud, referred to as "high fog." The fog in San Francisco is generally burned off by the morning sun.

San Francisco has two kinds of fog, wet and dry. The wet fog collects on trees and wires, forming large drops that fall to the ground, and windshield wipers are working furiously on automobiles. A dry fog may be equally dense but does not produce a drop of water, even though a driver may scarcely see a block ahead, and no moisture collects on trees. A dry fog is formed close by the shore and droplets have not had the opportunity to increase in size. The wetness of the fog is also affected by the temperature, with low temperatures making the fog wet and drippy.

The wet, drippy fog is normally the only kind of precipitation that reaches San Francisco in the summertime. Rainstorms approaching the California coast from the Pacific are blocked by the Pacific High, that mountain of cool, heavy air centered on the ocean a thousand miles or so offshore. The storms are forced to detour around the northern end of the Pacific High and strike the coast of Oregon and Washington instead.

Fog, or the absence of fog, is of constant interest to the fisherman. Heavy fog is an active and permanent menace to navigation. When the westerly wind weakens, it fails to cause the usual upwelling of cold water that create the fog and without this the ocean temperatures

rise. Many kind of fish normally found in the cold waters
of Northern California, including salmon and albacore,
migrate northward and are not found in the usual numbers
offshore. In their place, fishermen find quantities of fish
from the warm southern waters, barracuda, bonito and
yellow tail.

· There are several well marked types of fog in San
Francisco. First, and most prominent, is the summer
afternoon sea fog, which forms in the Gate. The second
is tule fog, a low-lying dense river fog which forms during
winter mornings and drain slowly seaward, about a mile
an hour. It is named from the tules, or bullrushes in the
Sacramento-Joaquin River beds. It is essentially a valley
fog, but sometimes forms early in the City, dissipating
under the warm sun before noon. The third type is more
familiar to big city residents, smog, a mixture of city
smoke and dust with condensed vapor.

It is the low-lying tule fog, more often than the
high fog, which closes in the entire Bay and sets off that
cacophonous symphony of fog horns, an ear shattering
din that sometimes rattles windows if you live near the
water and keeps some people awake. There are the famed
fog horns that monotonously give off those baritone "eeh
. . . oh!" sounds. The dissonant chorus of some 30 fog
signals in the Golden Gate is set off with the first approach
of fog, but only 13 of them are within hearing of the
San Francisco shore.

Fog horns are pretty much taken for granted in
San Francisco. Old timers say once you get used to a
fog horn, and hear it through a long period of time, you'll
wake up when it stops. Not so to many visitors and out-
of-towners.

Whatever the reason, fog horns are usually thought
of as music to many San Franciscans, and generally most

all fishermen and seafarers. Old salts around the Bay can identify and pinpoint the fog signals by their pitch and tonal qualities. Fog-blinded navigators new to these waters must rely on the "Pacific Coast Light List," published by the Coast Guard. This manual explains the rhythmic patterns and characteristics of each signal.

There are three types of fog signals, each which have their own distinctive pitch and rhythm. These are the siren, the diaphragm (air horn) and the diaphone. The sirens utter a contralto wail of a single pitch. The air horn produces a louder single pitched baritone blast. The diaphone can create a similar sound, but can also be adjusted in pitch and timing to create a variety of noises, including the classic blast and grunt signal, "eeh . . . oh!"

In terms of power the diaphone has no peer, and to make sure that everyone in San Francisco knows it the Coast Guard, which is in charge of fog horns, has one of the loudest right in midspan of the Golden Gate Bridge. As a comparison, the Market Street traffic rush hour will produce about 70 decibels on a noise meter, the din of a boiler factory about 100 decibels. But a diaphone, at maximum power, will send the sound guage needle to a shattering 200 decibels. San Francisco fog horns are guaged to be heard at a distance of a mile to a mile and a half.

The fog horn orchestra is dominated by the big diaphone in the mid-span of the Golden Gate Bridge, and another on the south tower. Others are located at Fisherman's Wharf itself, the Embarcadero, the Bay Bridge, Alcatraz, Yerba Buena Island and Point Diablo and Lime Point on the Marin Shore. These fog horns are automatically set off by the 12th Coast Guard District when visibility drops to less than five miles at the mouth of the Bay and less than two miles inside. Coast Guard lookouts and civilian watchmen in lighthouses, shore stations and waterfront offices keep the vigil, guage the fog's density and then the switches are turned on to sound the regular warnings.

For a classic explanation of what makes a fog horn blow, the Coast Guard has issued the following legalistic and technical explanation of its loudest sea signal:

"The diaphone is an instrument, using compressed air for producing sound. It is essentially a cylindrical slide valve, reciprocated by a very efficient self-governing air motor. The slide valve alternately opens and closes ports through which air is discharged, in puffs, into a resonator to produce a very distinctive sound familiar to all mariners."

Actually, San Franciscans and its many visitors have to be thankful for all small favors when it comes to fog horns. Back in the old days, in 1856, a cannon was fired regularly as a warning of foggy weather from the Point Bonita Lighthouse, near the entrance to the Golden Gate. The military order of that day specified that the cannon should be fired every half hour when the fog was present and loud enough to be heard by all, and it was. There were 278 hours of fog during the first two months the cannon guardian was on duty, and the keeper virtually collapsed from exhaustion. The cannon was eventually replaced with a bell, operated by clockwork.

When one considers that San Francisco has an average of 1,000 hours of fog a year, it would appear to be an improvement to have the foghorn blues as background music rather than a window shattering cannon every half hour.

One of the area's local musicians even composed an aria based on the rhythmetic sounds of San Francisco's sea signals, called "Fuque for Five Foghorns." It did not achieve lasting fame. How could it, when the song could be heard each day played by the real symphony.

Chapter 11

CABLE CAR RIDE TO
FISHERMAN'S WHARF

*T*he ride to Fisherman's Wharf from the heart of downtown San Francisco is aboard one of those brave, sturdy, colorful and charming cable cars. The passengers are brave and sturdy and the rickety pre-1900 relics are colorful and charming.

The green and cream colored cable cars, adequately marked "Fisherman's Wharf," load up at the equally famed intersection of Powell and Market streets, the locale of that hump-backed turntable where passengers help push America's only truly workable transportation toy onto the circular wooden section in the middle of the street and take turns pulling what seems like the whole street around for the car's return trip.

These old cable cars sweep you light heartedly up the steep grade of Powell street, rattling and creaking its persistent way past Union Square, up the 23 per cent grade of California street and Nob Hill, down past the outskirts of Chinatown where one gets an unparalleled view of the Bay, and then one is catapulted around the bend, the only warning being a shouted jargon that sounds like this:

"Luk-od-fad-a-kuv!"

What the conductor is saying is "Look Out for the Curve." The more humane will make it simply, "Corner . . . Hang onnnnnn!" Once you survive that roller coaster section the rest is easy as the car passes through a pleasant neighborhood section, makes a long sweep across North Beach and then heads toward the pungent aroma of tangy sea air and Fisherman's Wharf.

The cable car ride in San Francisco is a thrill as well as cause for sheer terror as the car jauntily tops a summit and then heads full force down one of the city's steep hills. But, don't worry about all this, you will get to Fisherman's Wharf okay. What's more, you will enjoy the ride. The conductors are friendly, so are the other passengers who in their nervousness want to talk to somebody and the gripman will put on a show for you by clanging the bell on the roof to a merry tune.

San Francisco's cable car system numbers 39 cars, in two styles, of which only 23 operate at one time. There are 27 of the green and cream color, half ending at Fisherman's Wharf and the other half at Victorian Square, several blocks away down the waterfront at a turntable park with quaint benches and 19th century gas lights reminiscent of another era. The other 12, in red and gray and unique because grips at each end allow them to run either way without turning around, run up and down California street, between Market and Van Ness, a short run sometimes described as going from noplace to nowhere. To keep things running, the cable car system employs 200 highly trained people, not including Lynda Bird Johnson Robb. She was named an honorary conductor after being unceremoniously ousted from a cable car while eating butterscotch ice cream—a clear case of meeting up with a wrongly flavored conductor.

It also used to be that women were not allowed to stand on the running board of cable cars, an enforceable

Cable Car Ride to the Wharf
(Convention Bureau Photo by Ted Needham)

tradition as far back as memory goes, and many a time cars were summarily halted while ambitious females were ordered inside. This rule finally ended when a coed from the University of California at Berkeley, well trained in the protest movement, boarded a cable car at the busy intersection of Powell and Market and refused to budge from her stand on a running board. Traffic was jammed for blocks until she was finally arrested, and her photo spread over the front pages of newspapers.

The City Attorney studied his law books and reluctantly admitted there was nothing in the law that said women cannot stand on the running boards of San Francisco's cable cars. Women are still allowed to sit on the bench seat outside, a tradition in these days of mini skirts and crossed legs, visible to all spectators along the way, that will probably continue to be maintained, law or no law.

There are 140 employees known as "platform men," divided into gripmen, or operators, and conductors. The gripman's duties are two fold, making the car go and making it stop. That is not as simple as it reads, for he must have the tensile strength to pull a 280-pound grip and take 25 working days of unrelenting training to wrestle a stubborn piece of iron, and its companion brake, in the likes and manner to make any physical contortionist quite proud. The conductor collects fares and wrestles with a rear wheel brake on steep grades in as spectacular a manner as the gripman himself. Sixty mechanics, especially trained, work either on the cars themselves or keep the massive cable system and its powerful winding gears in shape.

Cable cars are the oldest regular transit form in service in the nation today, dating its birth back to August 1, 1873 in San Francisco. They operate on a principle as basic as taking hold of a rope and being pulled. Cars climb hills, cross flatlands or descend inclines by merely holding tight to a continually revolving motor-propelled cable in a slot underneath the ground in the center of the tracks.

The grip that holds this cable is in front of the car and the adjustable crotch of the grip acts as fingers in clutching onto the cable to be pulled forward. The further back the hand lever is pulled the stronger hold the grip has on the cable and the faster the car goes, up to a speed officially estimated at 9 miles an hour. This ridiculous figure is more generously estimated at between 15 and 20 miles an hour by experienced riders.

There are three separate brakes on each cable car. The wheel brakes, consisting of metal "shoes" are applied to front wheels by a foot pedal and to back wheels by a conductor operated winding crank in the rear of the car. Track brakes consist of pine wood blocks situated between the wheels. Operated by hand lever, the wood blocks bear down on the tracks when applied and help bring the car to a halt. These wood blocks are replaced every two or four days.

The emergency brake is a guillotine-shaped metal wedge operated by a red hand lever, and is to be used only in emergencies. When applied, the wedge penetrates the cable slot, forcing the car to cease running with a body jolting stop that has been known to send riders to a hospital for treatment. So effective are these brakes that a welding crew is required to release the car from its stopped position after it is used.

The cable itself, running under the ground with a loud humming sound, is constructed in six strands of 19 wires each, with a manila rope core. Interestingly enough, this cable is a continuous one and four cable lines figure-eight their way through massive winding wheels in the cable car barn power house, running across suspension pulleys to tension carriages and back to their underground slots extending 10½ miles. There is a 750 horsepower motor which runs the cable.

San Francisco's cable cars were the brainchild of Andrew S. Hallidie, an English born Scotsman who arrived

in America with his father to spend his early years
specializing in cable making. As the story goes, one fog-
bound night in 1869, as he returned home via Powell
street he watched an overloaded horse-drawn passenger
carriage in trouble. Unable to bear the weight, the horse
slipped on the damp street, and down went carriage,
passengers and all screaming to the bottom of the hill.

Determined to halt unnecessary cruelty and death
of overworked carriage horses, Hallidie decided it was
time to put his cable to practical use and developed a
cable grip to carry passengers in horseless cars up the
steep San Francisco hills. With the help of friends, and
much of his own money, Hallidie got the city to grant
him a franchise.

In the early morning hours in 1873, Hallidie and his
friends mounted their horseless carriage to his primitive
screw-type grip on the top of one of the steepest hills in
San Francisco, on Clay street. He and his friends picked
up the cable and up and down the steep hill they went.
At the bottom they shook hands gleefully and clapped
each other on the back. The damned thing worked.

So successful was the Hallidie operation that within
the next 20 years some nine more cable companies were
formed, and nearly 600 cars were in operation on the
City's hills. The City was happy with the cars, the
passengers were happy and the crews were happy. So
were the youngsters of the day. Fun for them was linking
bent wire through slots in the ground and latching onto
the cable while on roller skates and ride precariously up
the hill and then plummeting to the bottom on their own
power.

With the advent of electricity and electric cars, many
of the cable car lines were rendered useless, but life was
relatively peaceful for the surviving cars until after World

War II when the war years took their toll by throwing tracks, cables and cars into disrepair.

In 1947, city officials announced they would abandon the entire cable car system, citing deterioration and progress as an excuse. It is more than likely that would have been the end but for a wisp of a charming public spirited physician's wife, Mrs. Hans Klussmann. She mobilized an army of determined volunteers, including such notables as Irene Dunne, Katherine Cornell, Sigmund Romberg and Lawrence Tibbett, and there began one of the most flamboyant, persistent and table pounding battles against city officials in modern San Francisco history.

In five separate political clashes, spanning 1947 to 1954, Mrs. Klussmann's "Citizens Committee to Save the Cable Cars" outmaneuvered and outfought city hall bureaucrats intent on stripping San Francisco of her cable cars, including a court victory that required one city official to give up part of his salary for campaigning against the cable cars on city time. "To me," said Mrs. Klussmann, "stopping the cable cars would have been like ripping the heart out of the City." Mrs. Klussmann finally won a near-pyrrhic victory in 1954 when she obtained enough signatures for an initiative on the ballot and voters overwhelmingly approved an amendment written into the City Charter guaranteeing perpetuation of the existing lines. In the seven year siege, however, the system had lost 50 per cent of its cars, having shrunk to its present miniscule size.

The justification of Mrs. Klussmann's fight was confirmed in 1964 when the National Park Service in Washington, D.C., impressed by the car's historical significance and uniqueness, designated cable cars a national landmark. The beloved institution of the cable car is further immortalized in story and verse. You can buy a hobby kit and put the pieces together and have a model cable car. Florist shops sell glazed pottery models suitable for centerpieces, jewelers sell miniature sterling silver cable cars for charm bracelets and many prominent San Franciscans give out cable car cuff links as gifts.

Today the cable car remains as an unique part of San Francisco, a prime tourist attraction, and the source of many humorous tales, such as this one recited by Columnist Herb Caen:

One of the Powell Street cable cars had difficulty arriving at Pine street. The car started up the grade and near the intersection the conductor appropriately shouted: "Pine street," just as the grip started to slip and the car slid silently down the hill. The gripman tried again and as the car approached the intersection the conductor bawled out: "Pine again." Once more the car started sliding downhill. This time the more chivalrous passengers got off and lent a hand from behind, pushing and shoving, and as the car finally made the grade the conductor shouted triumphantly:

"For the third and last time, Pine street!"

Chapter 12

BENNY BUFANO'S STATUE

*A*s you depart from the cable car and walk down Taylor street towards Fisherman's Wharf, you will pass a handsome 18 foot, 12½ tons giant granite statue of St. Francis of Assisi standing erect on the grounds of the International Longshoremen's and Warehousemen's Union. The statue shows the saint with his arms flung out in graceful benediction. Into the face is carved the forgiveness that St. Francis showed towards those who, as he was dying, betrayed the meaning of his mission.

The innocent looking statue, completed in 1933 in Paris and now resting a short block from the center of Fisherman's Wharf, has a history that makes it perhaps one of the most martyred religious statues in history. The late English critic Roger Fry called it "the most significant piece of sculpture done within 500 years." The statue has had, however, as restless a career as the sculptor himself, Beniamino ("Benny") Benvenuto Bufano, a fiery San Francisco sculptor who has been described as one of the most talented sculptors in this century.

Bufano, who was born in 1898 in San Fele, a village south of Eboli in Southern Italy, has not only become a great sculptor but a man of peace and a citizen of the world. He was born of Italian parents and his grand-mother was of Jewish descent.

In his time he walked with presidents and princes. He worked as a coolie on the docks in Canton, slept with the savages in their native huts in Africa, lived a purposeful life in Israel, walked by the side of Mohandas Gandhi and fought with the revolutionist Sun Yat-sen in China.

Bufano's father, a one-time governor of Basilicata Province in Italy and a follower of Garibaldi, fled to this country in 1901 as a political refugee, bringing a family of 16 children, of which Benny was the next to youngest. At 10, Benny became an apprentice to a wood carver in New York, where the family settled. From this humble start he soon won scholarships to art schools and learned to draw, paint and sculp.

In 1915, the young Bufano came to San Francisco to execute some designs for the exposition of that year. It was the start of a long career of controversy and public battles. Bufano yelled publicly that he never got paid. The exposition people said they gave his boss $500. During World War I, Benny, who was a pacifist, cut off the tip of his trigger finger and sent it as a protest to President Wilson.

Even in his later years, Benny was not reticent in expressing his opinions publicly. He argued with a mayor of San Francisco and exploded with: "You are stupid!" He fought with his fellow teachers in an art school and quit after he told the faculty: "The whole bunch of you ought to be selling bananas!" He was appointed once to the City's Art Commission by a benevolent mayor who should have known better. Bufano argued that the other commissioners should have been fired because they knew nothing of art. He was not re-appointed.

Bufano's trademark has become massive statues of St. Francis. His use of stainless steel will probably stand

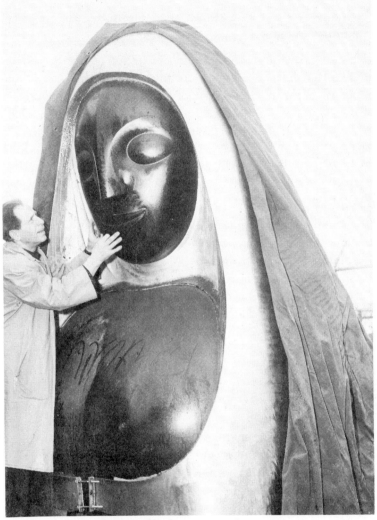

Benny Bufano and Statue

as a landmark in the history of sculpture. He executed a series of three giant murals for a downtown cafeteria, who then presented him with his fee as well as a lifetime meal ticket. He made the black granite statue of Tombstone the cat, the mascot of the Press Club and his famed

14-foot statue of Sun Yat-sen stands in the square opposite St. Mary's Church.

The tiny and temperamental genius, only 5 feet 2 inches tall, has always had trouble keeping his hands on money. "I want to be poor," said Benny, "because I want to make my statues for the poor and not the rich who put them in fancy homes where no one sees them." Benny also said he makes them big so that they couldn't fit in private homes. On another occasion he had a more plausible explanation: "I make my statues big to express the power and immensity of God."

Benny's troubles with the St. Francis of Assisi statue began when he carved the giant statue out of Perdurable Belgian granite when he was in France in 1933, living in LaVarenne St. Hilaire, a suburb of Paris. The stone-cutting and chiseling took him two years, and another month to work on details. Then he ran into troubles with his creditors and the French government. Benny owed $2,500 for payment of the granite and the statue rested in a warehouse which the government wanted to make into a railroad depot. The French government threatened to confiscate and sell the statue, but nobody in France wanted to move 12½ tons of granite, let alone buy it. The government finally decided to forget it and built its depot elsewhere, and Benny left for San Francisco. All this came to the attention of Paul Verdier, a prominent Frenchman and civic minded San Francisco department store owner.

On one of his many visits to France, Verdier saw the statue, as did a number of other civic minded San Franciscans on visits to Paris. They were all struck by its beauty. To show the remarkable effect of the statue, it gathered dust for the next 22 years in that Paris warehouse, surviving World War II and the invasion and retreat of the German Army.

Neither Verdier and his small group of followers ever gave up, being as zealous as St. Francis himself when he made a pilgrimage to convert the sultan of Babylon in 1219.

The break in the long stalemate came in early 1955. Benny's creditors had long since forgotten, or were forgotten themselves, and the French government, tiring of the pressures by Verdier and the committee, agreed to give up the statue of St. Francis of Assisi. The committee then made an offer to the Archdiocese of San Francisco, which was accepted, and the statue was brought to its first and most natural home, the steps of the humble church of St. Francis of Assisi in the heart of the North Beach section of San Francisco.

There, on October 4, 1955, some 1,500 people of San Francisco crowded around the street to see the ceremonies and hear the Auxiliary Bishop of San Francisco, the most Reverend Merlin J. Guilfoyle, bless the statue. Benny was pleased, the church was pleased, and the people were pleased.

Five years later it was a different story. The church had a new pastor who disliked the work. He complained the statue blocked the way of parishioners, especially when there were weddings and funerals coming in and out of the church. Besides, the priest said, the statue's heavy tonnage was causing cracks in the concrete steps of the church. Another problem was the area's bearded artists who enjoyed sitting on the stairs beneath the welcoming arms of the saint, eating lunch and various snacks. The statue must go, said the priest. Bufano protested, again publicly, and civic lines were drawn between those who wanted the statue to stay and those who wanted it to go. The statue went.

While San Francisco slept, the fertile mind of Maynard Corlett, an Oakland real estate man, won out.

He got Benny to agree to move St. Francis to private
property, facing Franklin Square in downtown Oakland,
being dedicated again with considerable civic acclaim.
Unfortunately, the statue of St. Francis had been placed
in front of vacant quarters that were rented and the
new tenants found it couldn't open its front doors with
St. Francis in the way. The next stop for St. Francis was
the ignominious patio of Si's Charbroiler in Oakland. It
stood with its back to a cocktail lounge, its hands blessing
customers sitting under gaily colored umbrellas eating
hamburgers. "We like it," said Owner Simon Furman,
"After we got it, business was good." Business was good
for 18 months, after which the ILWU union persuaded
Benny to move his statue to a permanent resting spot at
Fisherman's Wharf. Not only that, said the ILWU, but
the statue would be located in a tiny park setting and
would contain a base of water for birds, because St.
Francis loved birds.

"This is the end of the divine comedy," said Benny
in relief. "St. Francis will now be happy."

The statue symbolized something different to the
union than it had to others through the years. "The statue
captures the feeling that most of us feel towards our
union," said one official. "It's a feeling of warmth and
welcome and brotherhood."

So in December of 1962 the well travelled symbol
of peace was moved from Oakland to its new resting
place at Fisherman's Wharf, with the sculptor nestled in
the arms of his well padded masterpiece aboard a huge
flat bed truck. "I was so happy that it was coming home
that I had to ride with it," said Benny.

Chapter 13

THE ROCK OFF FISHERMAN'S WHARF

*S*itting grandiosely in the middle of San Francisco Bay is a 22-acre rock known as Alcatraz Island, so close to Fisherman's Wharf that on a clear day it seems one can almost reach out and touch the shores of that forbidden island.

If the city fathers of San Francisco would have had the choice, in 1934 when the Federal Bureau of Prisons announced the island would become a maximum security penitentiary, to decide beforehand if they wanted the world's most notorious prison in their backyard they would almost certainly have shouted an overwhelming no.

Four years later it was another matter.

By then, to the amazement of all and to the astonishment of civic and business organizations who had protested violently against "that blot, that hell hole in our Bay," The Rock proved to be a magnificent tourist attraction. It did not hurt the business at Fisherman's Wharf as so many had feared. People flocked to Fisherman's Wharf by the hundreds to get a distant glimpse of a place they would have hated to set foot on.

Batteries of high powered telescopes were mounted at Fisherman's Wharf to supply a somewhat closer view of its forbidding superstructure and massive cream colored buildings. Special harbor tours by boat, packed with sight seers, circled the bleak little island for a closer look yet. Every day yachts and pleasure craft moved closely past the island on their way to fun and games. The picture postcard industry joined the chorus with colorful reproductions of the island for visitors to send back home to friends inscribed with a caption: "Having Wonderful Time—Wish You Were Here!"

Alcatraz Island has been chartered on the maps of the world for more than 400 years, having been first discovered in 1545 by a detachment of Spanish troops exploring California. The honor of naming the island goes to Don Juan Manuel de Ayala, a lieutenant of the Royal Spanish Navy, commanding the survey ship *"San Carlos"* on a tour in August, 1775. He spotted the island with a living layer of pelicans and christened it "Isla de los Alcatraces," Island of the Pelicans. As often the case, it turned up misspelled "Alcatraz" on an 1862 map, and the name remained.

It hardly seemed a likely place to become world famous. The island did not then, or today either, contain a drop of fresh water, it had no vegetation and its rocks —rising 136 feet above sea level at its highest point— were dangerously steep cliffs and offered no shelter for ships. To complete the melancholy picture the island lay exposed to almost permanent cold winds, which in moments of calm are replaced by fog, keeping the temperature at a year round shivering level.

Nothing much happened to Alcatraz until the next century. The entire Bay area's population numbered only a few thousand souls who had all the elbow room they needed, and no desire to compete with fog bound pelicans. In those days Alcatraz, and California, belonged to Mexico. Pio Pico, the last Mexican Governor of California whose name is immortalized by a fashionable Mexican restaurant next to Fisherman's Wharf called "Senor Pico," was a politician who found land grants a convenient way of satisfying his creditors. In April, 1846, Governor Pico was being hounded by a persistent creditor, a local American named Julian Workman. He satisfied the claim by granting Workman the rights to Alcatraz, though why Workman wanted the island nobody ever found out. He was never known to have set foot on it.

In June of the same year the Bear Flag revolt erupted in California, finished Mexican rule in San Francisco, and gave Workman and others things more important than Alcatraz to worry about. Workman then "conveyed" the island to his son-in-law, named Temple; in turn Temple "conveyed" it to the newly installed Governor John C. Fremont for $5,000, which Temple claimed he never received; and Governor Fremont conveyed it to the banking firm of Palmer Cook & Co., who in turn conveyed it to the government of the United States on behalf of Fremont. All this was a fine kettle of fish which legal minds to this day have been trying to untangle.

As late as May of 1964, Ramsey Clark, then Assistant U.S. Attorney General, made a lengthy ruling for U.S. Senator Edward V. Long's Judiciary Committee that Alcatraz didn't belong to members of the Sioux Tribe either, who suddenly decided to lay claim to Alcatraz on the basis of an 1868 treaty, or to anybody else. Many of Governor Pico's land grants were invalid anyway, said Clark, so nobody but the United States ever owned Alcatraz.

The first installation on Alcatraz was a lighthouse in 1845. In March, 1853, Congress voted $500,000 for San Francisco's harbor defenses and eventually $2,000,000 was spent to equip the island with three batteries of heavy guns, water cisterns, bomb proof shelters and a guardhouse. By 1858, The Rock had been transformed into Fort Alcatraz and manned by 130 gunners. The process of The Rock developing as a place to confine prisoners

came gradually. It started with drunks and deserters
being locked up. Alcatraz was a formidable fortress by
any standard and would certainly have given any enemy
attacking San Francisco a bad time. But no enemy ever
came and as the importance of its guns declined, that of
its guardhouse grew. In 1868, Alcatraz was designated
by the Army departmental commander as a place of confinement for prisoners with long sentences. During the
Indian Wars of the 1870s and 1880s the island was found
useful as well as a secure place of confinement for rebel-
lious Indian leaders. During the immediate aftermath
of the Spanish-American War the island was used for
court-martialed soldiers.

Following this, for some reason, the island was then
used as a convalescent center for men returning from the
Philippine Islands with dysentry. Perhaps the idea of a
civilian prison started in 1906, when the San Francisco
earthquake and fire made it necessary to remove prisoners
from the local jail and lodge them temporarily on Alcatraz.
World War I brought conscientious objectors to Alcatraz
for discipline. Finally, the military tired of the cost and
let the island deteriorate until history changed the course
of events in 1934.

The tail end of Prohibition, combined with the peak
of the Depression, gave rise to an era of unbridled gang-
sterism. Notorious hoodlums were put in state prisons,
but refused to stay. John Dillinger engineered the famed
escape of 10 of his pals from Indiana State Prison, and
himself was freed by friends from a jail cell four months
later. The warden at Lansing State Prison was taken
as a hostage during a prison break. The climax came at
Kansas City when a carload of gangsters tried to liberate
one of their members being transferred to another prison,
killing four officers and wounding two FBI men.

It was against this background that the Department

of Justice decided on January 1, 1934, to take over Alcatraz to hold the Public Enemies after the FBI caught them. Attorney General Homer Cummings announced that the new prison would be as "escape proof" as human beings could make it. It would be the American version of Devil's Island.

Nature aided the government as well. The tides swirled past the island at from six to nine knots and the winds varied from 4 to 25 miles an hour. The water was usually a bone-chilling 51 degrees and the U.S. Army at the Presidio watched the nearby land while the U.S. Coast Guard patrolled the nearby waters. Alcatraz became something else at the start. It became a place without privileges, no trustees, single cells for every prisoner, no honor system and no entertainment. There were 100 guards for 262 prisoners and no favors. Originally there was also a "Rule of Silence," forbidding convicts to talk at meals and cutting them off entirely from the outside world. The only time this was broken was when the warden pinned the news of the attack of Pearl Harbor on the notice board. To evade the silence rule, the inmates developed a side-of-mouth mutter that became a trademark of gangster performances by James Cagney and Humphrey Bogart.

The noted gangsters who came to the Golden Gate and were transferred in the early morning hours through the chilly waters to the new island prison gave San Francisco and Fisherman's Wharf a new status in a crime-lore-satured nation. One of the first inmates at Alcatraz was the notorious Al Capone, Chicago beer baron and gangland chief. He was joined there eventually by such bank robbers, kidnappers and killers as Alvin Karpis, George R. "Machine Gun" Kelly and Basil "The Owl" Banghart. Between 1934 and the closing of the penitentiary in 1963 more than 1,500 such men were transferred to Alcatraz.

But the most famous prisoner of all brought to Alcatraz was perhaps the most pathetic. He was Lifer No. 594, Robert F. Stroud, the "Birdman of Alcatraz," who spent 54 years in prison, 43 of those years in solitary confinement. During those years Stroud spent 17 years in solitary at Alcatraz and his story was immortalized in book form by writer Thomas E. Gaddis and in a prize winning film starring Burt Lancaster.

San Francisco spent many uneasy days during the time that Alcatraz held the crime spotlight. The Federal Commission on the Disposition of Alcatraz Island in 1964 concluded this in their study: "The island penitentiary, perhaps because of the very notoriety of many of its charges, became the subject of many unwarranted rumors." But many of the events that shook Alcatraz were not rumors. At least 35 men tried to escape. Altogether three guards and ten convicts died in escape attempts and subsequent executions.

The most spectacular escape attempt came in 1946. Seven cons, with guns seized from guards, tried shooting their way out. Before the subsequent three-day battle ended, 100 battle dressed Marines and as many San Francisco police, were joined by five Coast Guard boats, two Navy vessels, a police launch and a military plane. The frightening battle off Fisherman's Wharf, with the explosions of grenades and shells clearly visible on shore, left five dead and 15 wounded.

The many escape attempts and the obvious futility of maximum security Alcatraz as a crime deterrent brought about the closing of The Rock in April of 1963. Attorney General Robert F. Kennedy cited the high maintenance cost of $13 per day per prisoner and the prospects of a $5,000,000 bill for repairs and signed the order. Most of the prisoners were transferred to a new $10,000,000 maximum security prison at Marion, Illinois.

Alcatraz Island, at this writing, lies abandoned. There are about 25 buildings in various states of decay and only the gray sea and the creeping white fog and the lights of a great city across the water pay attention to Alcatraz. The cost of constructing any new projects on the island would be formidable. It will cost at least $1,500,000 merely to demolish the present structures, and another $1,500,000 to barge the material away.

What will be done with Alcatraz Island remains to be seen. The Alcatraz Island Commission, authorized by Congress in 1964, held public hearings and studied 500 different proposals. The Commission recommended a monument be built to honor the founding of the United Nations in San Francisco in 1945 and become a symbol of peace. The Commission said the monument should be selected by an international panel from international architectural competition and funds would be raised by a private organization. The report is filed and gathering dust in Washington.

The Commission did have one important comment which will surely be wholeheartedly and firmly endorsed by a majority of San Franciscans.

"Under no circumstances," the Commission said, "should anyone be allowed to use the island to glorify the criminal acts which brought men to Alcatraz or to exploit the human misery associated with crime."

Chapter 14

THE GOLDEN GATE BRIDGE

*L*ooking westward from Fisherman's Wharf one can plainly see two majestic towers of deep chrome red steel rising into the sky and standing like a lonely sentinel spanning the waters of the Golden Gate, the traditional gateway to the Orient. Stretching past these two towers of steel is a roadway that appears as a black horizontal line and looping down from the towers, two perfect parabolas of cable. It is one of the dramatic sights that reward diners at Fisherman's Wharf.

This is the ethereally beautiful Golden Gate Bridge, rising in defiance of nature to cross the turbulent entrance of the Bay from the City's northernmost point to the rocky tip of Marin County. Completed in 1937 at a cost of $35,000,000 it is one of the world's longest and highest single-span suspension bridges. Fog enshrouds it, artists paint it, photographers picture its beauty from every angle, and suicides find it irresistable.

No previous bridge has had to compensate for so many troubles and problems, and no previous bridge was ever plagued by so much controversy, the effects of which continue to this very day. It is remarkable alone in that it was built completely without Federal financial aid, a statement in this day and age that will bring raised eyebrows of respect. After the California legislature authorized a Bridge District with power to build the bridge, it took six years of legal battle before the U.S. Supreme

Court permitted it to proceed. The War Department debated a year before giving its permission, fearing that destruction of the bridge during a war would block the harbor. Certain civic groups and business organizations greeted the proposal with ridicule, astonishment and cries of outrage.

In opposition were ferryboat operators, who then dominated cross Bay traffic and were afraid of being put out of business, a fear that later came true; and many shipping interests who thought the bridge would interfere with ship traffic, a groundless fear. Opposition came from 13 engineers, including the City engineer of San Francisco, who signed statements criticizing the project. Well meaning conservationists distributed literature and cartoons fighting "against the destruction of nature."

"Don't you think it wrong for any man to build anything that will mar God's beauty," asked one charming matron at a public hearing. Quietly the speaker looked over the well proportioned lady and answered:

"Madam, you have a man made product protecting your bosom but it has not marred God's beauty."

An eminent geologist from Stanford University, noting that the bridge would be parallel to the San Andreas fault whose 22-foot shift in 1906 levelled San Francisco, predicted the rocks holding the south end of the bridge were unstable and would crumble.

Much of this imposing opposition might have had its effect but for bridge advocates led by Engineer Joseph B. Strauss, who probably more than any one man is given credit for building the now world-renowned bridge. He carried on a 15-year crusade on behalf of his ambition. Strauss was a specialist in long span bridges and since he first saw its possibilities in 1917 he dreamed of the day when he would tackle "the most difficult engineering feat ever faced." Strauss was Napolean sized, just over five feet tall, and a persistent crusader for engineering progress.

He was an inventor, innovator, promoter, a shy introvert, but above all he was a great engineer. At one time or another he developed plans for a tubeless tire, a room cooler, a railroad freight car made of concrete, a glass washing machine for soda fountains and a railroad crossing guard that would catch an automobile in an elastic net and spring it back gently from an approaching train. He even wrote poetry. But, bridges were his business and he built nearly 400 in the United States alone. He also spanned waters in Egypt, Japan, South America and China. For the czar of Russia he built a bridge across the Neva River to reach the winter palace.

Progress could not be denied and construction began on the Golden Gate Bridge on January 5, 1933—14 years after Engineer Strauss had selected the site and 26 months after voters of six counties had approved the span's financing. Unique by any description, the bridge was financed by municipal bonds. The bridge is controlled by a quasi-municipal corporation and its directors are private citizens appointed by county supervisors. That means political appointments and no one really expected the raging controversy to end once construction started.

California bankers were hesitant to buy the bonds to finance the bridge until a historic meeting between Engineer Strauss and the noted banker A. P. Giannini of the Bank of America. It was a meeting of two men of vision. "San Francisco needs that bridge," Giannini replied simply. "We will take the bonds." Progress began on the construction front. The controversy moved to the political front. The bridge district's first general manager came under repeated newspaper fire for money problems. He finally resigned. Following this, the bridge district's telephone operator was fired, then re-hired, in a com-

The Grandeur of the Golden Gate Bridge

(Photo by Cynthia Wallis)

plicated cause celebre in which the Attorney General of California was finally called in for a ruling. Her problem? She was not nice to other operators and hadn't bothered to distribute copies of complimentary letters.

Surviving this, nature had her turn on the bridge. In the struggle between man and sea during the first year of construction it looked as if the sea would win. One foggy August day, after eight months of preliminary work, an inbound freighter loomed out of the fog and plowed through a working trestle, sending 100 feet of it to the bottom. In November, heavy seas battered the rebuilt trestle, knocked off the working equipment at the end and sank three house-sized concrete blocks that were to have been used in the foundation. Then came real tragedy.

On February 17, 1937, workmen on a wooden platform beneath the girders were tearing boards from the underside of the hardened concrete floor. Suddenly a corner bracket snapped and the platform tore loose and fell, ripping away the huge safety net below it and sent 10 men to their death in the surging waters below.

One man, Tom Casey, a red-haired Irish carpenter, leaped as the planking fell away beneath him and caught a flange of one of the lowermost beams from which the scaffold had hung. There he dangled, his pipe still clenched in his teeth, before he was brought up. Safe on deck, he removed his pipe a little shakily and said, "Thanks, boys, that was a nice ride."

On its completion, 80,000 miles of cable wire were used, 254,690 cubic yards of concrete and 80,000 tons of structural steel. The steel for the two towers were rolled and fabricated in the East, shipped by rail to Philadelphia, then by water through the Panama Canal to San Francisco Bay.

The bridge has a total length of 9,266 feet. The two graceful towers are 846 feet high. When the sun expands the steel the towers will lean several feet and the two 36½ inch cables will lengthen 16 feet. The two towers are not solid. To make them flexible they are cut up inside into cells like a honeycomb, each cell being three and a half feet square and made from ⅞ of an inch steel plate. As an additional strength factor to make the towers earthquake proof, they are of split level construction and adjoining cells have different floor levels.

All these interior walls, floors and ceilings must be painted regularly. Steel ladders and small oval openings give access from cell to cell and a maintenance elevator, only three feet square, takes eight minutes to ride to the top. It is totally dark in the maze of cells and painters wear a battery-powered miner's lamp on their caps. For painters and watchmen who must prowl the 23 miles of ladder and cells, a 26-page booklet of directions has been printed.

Painting the bridge is a year-round job. Specially mixed to bridge requirements, the paint is called "international orange." It does not, however, leave the bridge orange at all, but more rust red, a vibrant shade that contrasts sharply with either blue sky or gray fog. To keep the bridge in its famous color, and more important to keep the span from rusting away, two tons of paint are used each week. Painters on the cables on top of the bridge climb up and down wearing non-skid shoes. To paint the vertical suspender ropes the men lower themselves from the cable on bosun's chairs. Painting on the undersize of the bridge is done by men walking on a wide scaffold suspended below the deck. Ninety per cent of all painting is done by hand brushes, because the wind would spread sprayed paint over the passing cars. The west side of the bridge is heavier than the east side because of the prevailing wind that blows off the ocean and necessitates a heavier coat of paint on that side.

The bridge opened officially at 6 a.m. on May 28, 1937, capping a week of gala civic ceremonies. The first day was reserved for pedestrians and Donald Bryant, a sprinter, was the first man across. Among others claiming firsts was the first person to cross on stilts, the first pair of twins, the first mother pushing a baby carriage and the first to cross walking backwards. There was always someone seeking a first off the bridge. People climbed the bridge for notoriety, stuntmen parachuted from it, others married on it and daredevils flew planes beneath it.

The bridge, like all high places, soon proved a fatal fascination for suicides and an average of 10 to 12 persons a year jump off the bridge. Coast Guardsmen at Fort Point manage to recover most of the bodies. The remainder are carried out to the Pacific on ebb tide, one of the most powerful in the world. Four and a half million cubic feet of water pour out of the Bay every second when the tide is strong—seven times the volume of the Mississippi at New Orleans.

None of this could stop the newspaper controversy over the years that constantly dogged the bridge's board of directors, and its succession of general managers. Grand juries on both sides of the Bay took turns at investigating charges of fraud. There were public battles over free bridge passes, a fight over how much to pay secretaries, over the need for a paid lobbyist, over expenditures for expense accounts and free life insurance for bridge directors.

The bridge came through World War II unscathed. During the war's long years they could report no instance of attack or sabotage. Not until the war was over did an incident stop traffic on the bridge. In June of 1946 a Japanese torpedo was found half buried in the sand of the Golden Gate, only a few hundred feet west of the bridge. Navy experts said it had been in the water for more than two years and probably drifted to shore from far out in the Pacific. The bridge was closed briefly to all traffic, charges were attached to the torpedo and it was exploded in a mushroom of flame, sand and smoke.

The bridge was closed again for a few hours in 1951 because of a violent, twisting wind that registered 70 miles an hour. It was shut down briefly again in April, 1960, when General Charles de Gaulle was paid a tribute offered none of the dignitaries who had crossed the bridge before him. The bridge was closed to all traffic except cars in his official motorcade. Although the French leader was given the personal use of the bridge, his car was treated just like any other. The driver had to pay the 25 cent toll.

In all the words ever written about the Golden Gate Bridge, and in all the discussions, there has always been the overriding subject of how long the engineering marvel of our time will stand. "Why, forever," was the assuring answer given by Engineer Strauss.

The foolish whispering campaigns when the bridge was first opened, and which unfortunately sometimes ended up in print, had it that the bridge might easily be destroyed by a violent storm, or by a few hundred men marching in step across the span, or that an orchestra might strike a certain chord and shake down the whole business. This is what Strauss had to say about all this.

"If the entire 4,200 feet of suspended span were jammed with loaded vehicles standing bumper to bumper in all the lanes, and if the sidewalks on both sides were crowded their full length with foot passengers standing shoulder to shoulder, if a 90-mile-an-hour gale were suddenly to hit the bridge—and if at that moment someone should saw the cable halfway through—why the Golden Gate Bridge would still stand!"

Chapter 15

THE SAILING SHIP "BALCLUTHA"

*L*ocated at Pier 43 at Fisherman's Wharf is the three-masted, square rigged sailing vessel *Balclutha,* the last of the old fleet of sailing vessels that braved their way around the Cape Horn to San Francisco from Gold Rush days to the time of the Panama Canal.

Glasgow-built, the *Balclutha* was launched in Scotland in 1886 as a merchant ship. She carried spice and jute from India, wheat from Australia and nitrate from South America to her home in England. At the turn of the century she changed her nationality to American and entered the Alaska run, carrying canned fish back to San Francisco. She was one of the last of the sailing ships on the Alaska run to be replaced by steam and she was retired in 1930. Three years later she was outfitted as a wax museum of pirates and for the next 19 years was a noted attraction, first at San Francisco's Fisherman's Wharf and later in the Long Beach area. While in Southern California the *Balclutha* augmented her income by taking part in nearly 40 movies, including the title role in "Mutiny On the Bounty." Then she came home to rest in the mud flats of Sausalito, across the Bay from Fisherman's Wharf.

Restored in 1955, the *Balclutha* now has a permanent home in San Francisco and has become a fond remembrance of a bygone era. The *Balclutha* has also become a classic example of the unbelievable patience and fortitude of a few heroic private individuals so that the color and romance of the sea might be made a permanent part of San Francisco lore for tourists and local residents alike.

The man almost single handedly responsible for this and other cultural maritime exhibits alongside Fisherman's Wharf is a mild mannered, heavyset man with thick glasses named Karl Kortum, who took to the sea after giving up a career as a chicken rancher at Petaluma, a town some 40 miles from San Francisco that calls itself the "egg basket of the world."

It started in March of 1949 when Kortum wrote an agonizingly long five-page letter, single spaced, to Scott Newhall, executive editor of the San Francisco *Chronicle*. Normally such letters are rarely read past the first page, or go to some non-caring reporter, but this one caused a stir. Kortum had first met Newhall a few months before when the State of California made a mistake and tried to ram a freeway through the Kortum property in Petaluma. Kortum asked Newhall for help and Editor Newhall who liked a fight as well as anyone, since he had also been an amateur boxer, joined the battle and the State gave up when they realized they had aroused a veritable wasps nest. Editor Newhall is a fighting editor out of the old school, and like the old school is noted for a variety of journalism coups. Newhall and the *Chronicle* later led the famed San Francisco freeway revolt, badgered the State into changing the design of a bridge, took on the Bay Area Rapid Transit system, the State's water plans and tilt their lances regularly at local corruption.

In 1936, Newhall took leave of his new job with the *Chronicle* to take the 42-foot ketch *Mermaid* on a leisurely trip around the world. It took him a year to get to Acupulco where he developed an infection in his leg which was ultimately amputated. He served later as a war correspondent with the Royal Navy in England and then came back to his job on the paper, rising to executive editor in 1952. He even ran later for Mayor of San Francisco.

Kortum's five page letter to Newhall thanked him and then began:

"It led me to think you and the *Chronicle* might be interested in a project of waking San Francisco up to its sailing ship tradition that has haunted me for 10 years. Unless I am mistaken, it is the stuff whereof a good newspaper campaign is made."

Editor Newhall sent the note through channels with his comments, noticeably briefer:

"The author is a stubborn and enthusiastic young man who sailed to Africa in 1941 with Hall. (Newhall's brother.) As you can see his one great passion is sailing. If anyone could put over the program he could. I would be glad to contribute any excess energy." Newhall's excess energy went so far as to later work on weekends to weld many ship models and to help restore the wiring on the *Balclutha*.

Kortum was indeed in love with the sea. He first built model ships, then built a skiff and learned to sail on Petaluma Creek, a salt water inlet. A cousin lent him a book filled with sketches of square-riggers and Kortum began to visit nearby ship graveyards, sleeping on decks and communing with the old sailing vessels. In 1935, when he read that the Japanese had bought many of the old ships tied up in the Oakland Estuary for scrap and that they planned to sail them across the Pacific, he applied to become a member of the crew. But the thrifty Japanese had brought over their own people. Kortum got his chance in 1941 when he left his poultry farm and sailed around the world on the *Star of Finland*, the last remaining American built square rigger. After the war,

Kortum began writing a book about his voyage and it was then that the State interrupted him with its freeway nonsense.

In his letter, Kortum suggested a vast project, so vast they simply called it "Project X." First he wanted a Maritime Museum and to go inside he suggested a fine collection of maritime artifacts, models and paintings that had already been assembled by a local shipping magnate, Edward S. Clark. They had later come under the sponsorship of Mrs. Alma de Brettesville Spreckels, the grand dowager of San Francisco. Then he wanted a transportation museum, a pier to dock old restored vessels, and finally to restore and bring back to San Francisco the *Balclutha*. Newhall was fairly bowled over, but the wheels began to move. City Hall agreed to cooperate, talk being cheap, and the City's newspaper editors backed the idea.

Getting the *Balclutha* was the first step. The 253-foot, 1,862 ton ship had gotten its name from Balclutha, the ancient Gaelic word for the site of Dumbarton, the home town where the original ship owner, Robert Mc-Millan, made his home. In the peak of the grain trade, one of the world's richest commerces in the 70s and 80s, no fewer than 560 sailing vessels similar to the *Balclutha* crowded San Francisco Bay waiting for grain cargoes. The *Balclutha* made her first voyage in 1877 from Cardiff to San Francisco, taking 12 months and six days for the voyage around the Horn. She rounded the Cape a total of 17 times as she discharged her homeward cargoes at Plymouth and London, and in the ancient ports of Amsterdam, Antwerp and Havre. She was then bought by San Francisco interests who owned sawmills on Puget Sound. She was put under the Hawaiian flag, after a special act of Congress, and sent north to Australia carrying lumber cargoes. Her cargo homeward was usually coal from Newcastle for locomotives of the Southern

Pacific Railroad. In 1904, she was wrecked near Kodiak Island and sold as she lay for $500 to the Alaska Packers Association. Refitted in 1906, and renamed the *Star of Alaska,* she sailed the Alaska salmon trade for 28 years.

She was then sold for $5,000 to Frank Kissinger, a Los Angeles showman who achieved some sort of fame by claiming to be the first man to drive a motorcycle around the inside of a giant barrel. Kissinger exhibited the ship at the San Diego Fair in 1935, then renamed her the *Pacific Queen* and camouflaged her as a pirate ship, complete with wax works of notorious pirates and buccaneers and even had planks to walk, and a steam calliope that could be heard for blocks. Kissinger brought her to the 1939 World's Fair at Treasure Island and then to Fisherman's Wharf where she was a popular attraction.

Then came World War II and the military shut down Fisherman's Wharf and Kissinger shunted his ship to Sausalito, where she lay until 1946. When Kissinger wanted to return to Fisherman's Wharf the State Harbor Commission refused, giving the odd reason that the ship attracted so many visitors before it created a parking problem. Kissinger then moved to the Long Beach area, which apparently didn't have a parking problem. Over the years the *Balclutha* deteriorated and in 1952 the old ship was towed to Sausalito and laid up in the mud flats. That is when Kortum entered the picture.

The *Chronicle* assigned a young reporter named David Nelson to work with Kortum. "The initial interest was high," said Nelson. "It was about as hard as selling $10 bills for $6.50." Then things got difficult and enthusiasm dwindled as the detail work grew. In 1952, owner Kissinger died, leaving the *Balclutha* to his widow Rose. By now, Kortum and the newspapers, led by Reporter Nelson, had formed a citizens committee which raised $20,000 to purchase the ship. Mrs. Kissinger proved to be a tough negotiator and talks dragged on for nearly a year. She wanted $25,000. Interest began to lag. The citizen's committee threatened to disband.

Finally, help came from Harry Lundeberg, then secretary-treasurer of the Sailors Union of the Pacific and probably the most powerful man on the waterfront. Kortum personally appealed for his help and he came through. Lundeberg's support revived interest and the persistent widow won out. The *Balclutha* was acquired for $25,000.

The problem of her restoration, which was expected to cost a quarter of a million dollars, was soon taken care of. Under the leadership of Lundeberg and Mario Grossetti, secretary of Local 9 of the Iron Shipbuilders Union, some 18 labor unions contributed 10,000 hours of free labor to the *Balclutha's* restoration and the shipping industry tossed in over $100,000 in goods and services. On July 19, 1955, after more than a year of work, the *Balclutha*, sparkling and renewed, was towed to Fisherman's Wharf and opened to the public. Acting Mayor Theresa McMahon broke a bottle of champagne on the *Balclutha* deck and a new life was begun for the ship, which its original owner said was built to last for 150 years, or until the year 2030.

And thus it was that Karl Kortum, the man with a warm appreciation of San Francisco's romance with the sea, summed it up as follows:

"All you have to have is an idea and the people who can carry it through."

Chapter 16

SAN FRANCISCO'S
$1,500,000 WHITE ELEPHANT

The Frenchy'd give his chapeau and
The Cockney'd give his whip
For a sight of San Francisco
From the Hyde Street grip.

Gelett Burgess

*F*or those readers not familiar with the late
California writer Gelett Burgess, they may recall this
more familiar couplet he wrote:

I never saw a purple cow,
I never hope to see one.
But, I can tell you anyhow,
I'd rather see than be one.

Like Burgess, a noted writer of sea stories, Karl
Kortum, the man who spearheaded the drive to bring the
Balclutha to Fisherman's Wharf, had taken the Hyde
Street cable car ride to the end of the line, coming to a
stop at the waterfront, three blocks from the Wharf.
Similar to its sister cable car line, which ends closer to
Fisherman's Wharf on another street, the Hyde Street
cable car starts its spectacular run at the Powell and
Market cable car turntable, past Union Square, Nob Hill
and then through Russian Hill and then down hill for
a dazzling view of the Bay at it comes to the end of
the line.

It was at the end of this ride that Kortum had his dream of seeing the Hyde Street cable car, which ended in a somewhat undistinguished manner at the end of the street, extended to a turntable of its own with a Victorian Park setting, a pier for restored vessels, a Transportation Museum and a Maritime Museum. That was quite a mouthful for anyone to chew, but Kortum was ready for big game. As the locale for his museum, which would be a living exhibit of San Francisco's romantic salt water past, Kortum chose a nearby padlocked building owned by the City. By doing so he sought to erase from memory a painful City experience, a $1,500,000 white elephant that had been left standing on its doorstep for everyone to see.

Kortum picked the lavish white Aquatic Park Casino at the foot of Polk street that had been lying dormant for 12 years. The dream of an Aquatic Park there had been kicked around for decades before ground was finally broken in 1935 by the Federal Works Progress Administration. The Casino was envisioned as a "palace for the public," a three-story futuristic bathhouse and a water playland for swimming and bathing. Ten thousand people a day were expected to stroll along a 1,800 foot curved seawall built to protect the basin, and thousands more would swim or else "sink into warm embracing sand imported for the purpose." Unfortunately, the planners had not taken into consideration the icy winds and clammy fog that blows in daily through the Golden Gate ten months out the year.

The project was destined for nothing but headaches. Three years later workmen were still there. Funds came in dribbles and construction was often interrupted for months at a time. Little by little, however, the building rose from the beach and soon it was a wonder to behold. The three-story white concrete structure was designed to resemble a streamlined battleship at anchor. It sparkled with glass and stainless steel fittings. At the beach level were vast dressing rooms where photo-electric showers automatically sprayed surprised bathers with chlorinated water, and dried them with blasts of warm air almost before they knew what was happening.

The main entrance on Beach street opened into a 100-foot ultra-modern lounge, glowing with dazzling murals of undersea life by Artist Hilaire Hiler. Assorted granite seals, penguins and frogs by Sculptor Benny Bufano carried out the marine motif. At either end of the lobby were two big circular chambers, the Rainbow Room and the Blue Room, appropriately decorated. On the floor above was a large banquet hall and above that a smaller Pilot Room, both flanked by sun decks looking out over the Bay.

City officials were anxious to take over the building from the WPA in time to have the dedication ceremonies on Mayor Angelo Rossi's 61st birthday on January 22, 1939. The Mayor's many Italian friends at Fisherman's Wharf were anxious to see the complex open to introduce their business to new visitors.

WPA officials were glad to get rid of the building, already a headache in which they had poured in $1,500,000 in a time when money was hard to come by. Over the protests of artists, who complained they hadn't finished the decorations, Federal officials turned the deed over to the City for $1 in time for the Mayor's birthday. Mayor Rossi was happy with the gift, but balked when photographers tried to get him to stick his bare foot in a block of wet concrete for historical purposes.

After its grand opening, the Casino really fell on bad times. A restaurateur who was given a concession in the building refused to pay his rent because his contract

The Historic Sailing Ships and a Historic Gas Lamp at the Foot of Hyde Street

(Convention Bureau Photo by Ted Needham)

with the City specified it would become effective only when the building was completed. The City took this problem to the WPA, but those officials refused to complete the art work as long as the building was being used for commercial purposes.

The dressing rooms at the Casino, built for 5,000 people, never accommodated more than 300 even on the few warm days when wind and fog subsided to make it pleasant at the beach. The water was too cold for bathers. The restaurateur went bankrupt. Then the final blow came when the Department of Public Health decreed that nearby sewage disposal made the lagoon unsafe for swimming. As a final touch much of the imported sand beach was swept away by tides, and discouraged City officials finally padlocked the building. If anyone feels that City Hall has improved over the years, the waters at the lagoon are still unsafe today for swimming because of the pollution problem. Kids being what they are, on warm days they swarm to the lagoon, disregard the "No Swimming" sign and paddle about. The City gave up trying to say no and finally, in its quixotic manner, assigned a life guard on duty there, and leaves standing its "No Swimming" sign.

During World War II, the Casino was taken over by the Army and used as a staging area in connection with adjacent Fort Mason. After the war the only activity around the Casino was a senior citizens recreation center in the Rainbow Room and weekend dances held by social clubs. On warm days scattered sun bathers lay on the lawn outside and occasionally patronized the dressing room and showers.

Again with the help of the City's newspapers, led by the indomitable *Chronicle,* and dozens of leading citizens, incorporated as a non-profit association in early 1950, the museum was opened to the public in May of 1951. The museum now contains a marvelous collection of figureheads, anchor blocks, nameboards, windlasses, wheels and ship models on the main floor. The second floor displays ship fittings, navigation instruments, sailors handcraft, early waterfront photos and pictorial histories of every type of vessel known to the port city. The musuem's steamship room has models of many well known modern ships.

Kortum having been installed as the museum director, had as an assistant a charming girl named Jean Edmonds, a young woman who had come to the City from Portland, Oregon, looking for a newspaper job, but ended up working at the museum. Kortum solved the problem of Miss Edmonds salary by marrying her. The museum was an immediate hit, but Kortum adjusted his glasses and began some new battles and in doing so fought the classic case against bureaucracy and entrenched civil servants.

The State Legislature had passed a bill in 1956 calling for a state park "somewhere on the San Francisco waterfront." That was Kortum's idea for the terminus of the Hyde Street cable car. State officials had the idea it would be in front of the nondescript Ferry Building, several miles away and in front of a concrete freeway. Kortum dictated press releases fighting the idea, even though he was technically a civil service employee himself, and had telegrams sent to everyone he could think of. He always signed the name of his friend, Harry Lundeberg, the powerful head of the Sailors Union of the Pacific.

Finally, in 1960, the State Public Works Board approved the expenditure of $175,000 and had built, where Kortum wanted it in the first place, an authentic Victorian Park which is now the turntable terminus of the Hyde Street cable car line. The pleasant park, created in the Victorian era motif, has old fashioned gaslights that really burn with gas, ornamental benches, tree guards, cast iron newel posts and a unique circular waiting station. It also has a name problem, but more of that later.

Next in line came the building of the Hyde Street Pier to contain four restored ships and in 1961 a 40-year lease was signed between the Park Commission and the State Port Authority, ending another long struggle. The ships now on display, three historic schooners and a walking beam ferryboat, was another part of Kortum's dream come true. The project of restoring an ancient warehouse for a transportation museum still goes on at this writing. How does this one-time chicken farmer accomplish these maritime miracles? It is easy, says Kortum.

"All you have to have is an idea . . .," he says.

Chapter 17

THE CHINA CLIPPER

*H*ow was it at Fisherman's Wharf in 1935? Hundreds lined the docks at Fisherman's Wharf and thousands more crowded the shoreline of San Francisco, stretching in a long thin line as far as the Marina, near the Golden Gate Bridge. It was late in the afternoon of November 22, 1935, and the crowds were waiting to see aviation history, the inaugural trans-Pacific flight of the 25-ton Pan American Airways airliner, the *"China Clipper."* The silvery craft, the largest airliner built to that date, its four gleaming Twin Wasp engines reflecting the mid-day sun, roared into action at 3:37 p.m. and skimmed across the waters for its take off from a dock at Alameda, where another crowd of more than 20,000 had gathered.

Eight years before, when Charles Lindberg soloed across the Atlantic in the *"Spirit of St. Louis,"* he had dreamed of the day when huge airlines would someday span oceans. This was part of his dream, because it was from specifications laid down by Colonel Lindberg that builder Glenn Martin had spent three years constructing the *"China Clipper"* at his Baltimore, Maryland, factory.

There were plenty of ceremonies and speeches to take up the slack of time when the crew of seven supervised the loading of 120,000 air mail letters, largely from stamp collectors anxious to get souvenir first-day covers of the first trans-Pacific mail. Later, the *Clipper* ship would

The China Clipper over S. F. Bay

begin carrying passengers to the Philippines and to China, where a few years ago men never dreamed of flying.

Messages were heard from California Governor Frank Merriam, Postmaster General James Farley, while Hawaii Governor Joseph P. Poindexter and Philippines President Manuel Quezon spoke by radio from Honolulu and Manila. President Franklin D. Roosevelt, describing himself as an "air minded sailor," sent the following message from Washington: "Even at this distance I thrill to the wonder of it all. There can be no higher hope than that this heritage of courage, daring, initiative and enterprise will be conserved and intensified."

The youthful PAA President, 37-year-old Juan Trippe, who had started his first airline in 1927 with tri-motored Fokkers on the run from Key West to Havana, set the stage for the takeoff.

"Today the first United States mail starts on a regular course destined for the Philippines, 8000 miles away," he said. "Succeeding schedules will be extended on to the coast of China. This is indeed a historical day."

Trippe then turned to the pilot, Captain Edward C. Musick, a veteran of 11,000 hours in the air. Musick was the first pilot hired by Trippe and in each case as a new route, or a new service, was inaugurated, it was he who was at the controls.

"*China Clipper*, are you ready?" asked Trippe.

"Ready and standing by for orders," said Captain Musick.

"Captain Musick, you have your sailing orders. Cast off and depart for Manila in accordance herewith."

The huge plane began its long taxi approach over the water and accompanied by cheers rose gracefully into the air, her silver wings reflecting the setting sun. The plane rose heavily towards the new San Francisco-Oakland bridge, then under construction, and dipped underneath the cables.

Climbing slowly to 800 feet the *China Clipper* came into view at Fisherman's Wharf and flew over a small flotilla of fishing boats and small craft. It swept by another crowd on the nearby shore where a program of more speeches, fireworks and cheering had been completed by San Francisco City officials, headed by Supervisor J. Emmet Hayden. Then the giant plane flew gracefully over the majestic Golden Gate Bridge and towards the Pacific on its first leg covering 2,400 miles to Honolulu. It was a most dramatic start of the longest over-water air mail service ever dreamed of.

What a strange contrast of time. More than 100 years ago the American clipper ship ruled the seas and the first one reached San Francisco and the waters off Fisherman's Wharf to open a new era of commerce. Now the most advanced airliner of the day was reversing the route, playing what was to be an even greater part in the adventure of mankind. One hundred years ago it was the native Indians who dominated the fishing waters, now it was the Italians .

What was life at Fisherman's Wharf like in 1935, when the new *China Clipper* ushered in a new era? This is the way it was described that year by veteran newslady Henriette Horak in the San Francisco *Chronicle*:

"Had the fire which threatened Fisherman's Wharf a few days ago not been checked, the leaping, hungry flames would have destroyed one of the show places of San Francisco—and once the favorite haunt of Enrico Caruso.

"The fishermen of Little Italy, who own the majority of the fishing fleet of more than 400 trim and gayly colored boats, love to tell tales about the famed tenor. How he brought his fellow countrymen the latest news from home and spent hours listening to stories of the sea told by the weather-beaten fishermen. They tell how more than once the famed tenor emptied his pockets to help pay for a new net, or for the mending of an old one."

(Enrico Caruso was a flamboyant and controversial personality, like getting fined $10 for pinching a young lady, and he was indeed a generous man. In the United States he would often meet fellow Italians in bad straits and end up pressing large sums of money into their hands, for he himself was born of a very poor family.

(Caruso was the most admired Italian operatic tenor of the Twentieth Century. He made his London debut in

1902 and in New York in 1903 and quickly developed an international reputation. He first came to San Francisco in 1905 to sing at the Mission Street Grand Opera House, after which he and other artists wandered through the then Fisherman's Wharf area. "He was in great spirits," wrote a reporter for the Italian language paper L'Italia, "and was manifested by a colorful assortment of Italian adjectives. As water flows from a faucet, so does the music from Caruso when he opens his mouth."

(The next visit to San Francisco for Caruso, who by then was renowned for his role of Canio, the clown, in "I Pagliacci," was in April of 1906, on tour with the Metropolitan Opera Company. The company opened the night of April 16 with "Queen of Sheba," which received luke warm reviews. The next night, April 17, Caruso bowled them over in "Carmen." Caruso and his friends celebrated with a tour among his fishermen friends on the wharf where the wine flowed freely over heaping platters of fish and spaghetti. Caruso, who was also a cartoonist of note, sketched comic drawings of himself on the tablecloth.

(The following morning, April 18, Caruso was sleeping soundly in his bed at the Palace Hotel when at 5:12 a.m. the earth shook and the sky fell with the earthquake and fire. Almost petrified with fright, Caruso donned his clothes and with a towel around his neck to protect his voice, and an autographed photo of President Theodore Roosevelt to protect his person, he made his way to safety. Six days later he reached New York and shouted to reporters: "Give me Vesuvias." He vowed never to return again to San Francisco—and he never did. Fifteen years later he finally agreed to sing in San Francisco, but he was struck down by pleurisy and died in Naples in August of 1912.)

Now continues the story of newslady Horak:

"For the fishermen at the Wharf to lose one of those henna-colored nets is a tragedy among the hard working paisanos. Since a thousand pounds of twine are necessary to make the largest net, and since the twine costs about a dollar a pound, the loss of a net is a costly item.

"A somber tragedy at Fisherman's Wharf in which the hero is still remembered in prayers and with lighted candles at Saints Peter and Paul, was told to us by one of the seasoned fishermen. His name was Pietro and he needed a new net. He saved his dollars until he had enough of them to buy several hundred pounds of twine. Night after night, after the day's labors, Pietro and his friends worked on the new net. Finally it was finished.

"Tomorrow Pietro would take his fine new net to the boat. What a handsome net it was, thought Pietro. Each strong knot just like the other. But, tomorrow never came for Pietro. The night before the momentous occasion fire broke out in Pietro's home.

"Pietro rushed into the burning dwelling to save his precious treasure, but in the excitement became entangled in the net and died in the flames.

"Fisherman's Wharf is a colorful spot. A descent down the west slope of Telegraph Hill, to the foot of Taylor Street, leads one to the bit of Neapolitan atmosphere. On the way one meets groups of dark skinned children breaking wooden boxes with an eager childish vengeance. And why not? Maybe Toni and Maria will get a nickel apiece for their piles of kindling, to buy a bottle of 'gazzoze' at the corner grocery. Divested of its Italian name, 'gazzoze' is nothing more than the ordinary soda pop, made in San Francisco by an enterprising young Italian.

"Both sides of Taylor are lined with fish stands of various sizes and architectural design. In front of each stand is stationed a strong-voiced barker, who extols the delights of his fish wares to the passer-by.

"A human landmark at the Wharf who provides much amusement for marketing housewives and the casual tourist, is an almost toothless joke of a man, harnessed to a tray of cigarets, 'gazzoze' and other small tidbits, and topped by a battered black derby which has that 'I have lived' look about it. 'I sold my shoes to buy some booze,' is the inevitable song of the never sober, grinning vendor. Nobody knows where he came from, but he is always there, and frequent visitors to the shore never fail to point him out as one of the shore curios.

"It is the crustacean (crab) that has put Fisherman's Wharf on San Francisco's map. Since to be at their perfection, crabs must be strictly fresh, they are brought to the Wharf alive and still kicking their objections. A combined circular stove and caldron graces the front of every fish stand. The crab-cocktail hungry tourist, or shopper, eyes the piles of squirming crabs, points to his favorite, and thus dooms him to a quick death in the boiling water. The once yellow crab, when plunged into the caldron, turns a mottled red color, gives a final jerk or two of protest, and in three minutes finds himself smothered in biting sauce—a crab cocktail!

"The shrimp comes a close second to king crab in cocktail popularity; while the lobster, clam, oyster, mussels, various kinds of fish, and yes, even the treacherous octopi hold their own among San Francisco's sea food fanciers.

"Hollywood screenstars have namesakes on Fisherman's Wharf. Gayly painted, tiny turtles, running amuck in shallow tanks—red ones dubbed Clark Cable; white, Mae West, and an atrocious purple, Wallace Beery. And how the tourists go for them!

"Friday is the busiest day on Fisherman's Wharf—
for Friday is the traditional fish-eating day and fish lovers
must be supplied with their favorite sea delicacies. Hundreds of conscientious housewives drive their cars to the
Wharf to personally select crab meat, oysters, tempting
strips of sole tenderloin and other gifts of the sea for
hungry husbands and children.

"And of course half the fascination of Fisherman's
Wharf, for most people, is the heavy smell of the sea and
its products which clings all over. It is a strange and
curious odor; the cool, bracing sea air, blended with the
hot, fishy steam of boiling caldrons, the none too pleasant
aroma arising from piles of slightly aged crab shells, and
hot grease under sizzling fish steaks. It is no smell for
the fastidious, but then, the fastidious have no business
on Fisherman's Wharf.

"Italians from all over America eventually find their
way to San Francisco, and to California, for it is here
that they find, as many have told us—'da sun, she is
warmer, ju-ust likka inna da olda countree!'"

That's the way it was at Fisherman's Wharf in 1935.

Chapter 18

JOE DI MAGGIO,
THE YANKEE CLIPPER

"I would like to take the great DiMaggio fishing," the old man said. "They say his father was a fisherman. Maybe he was as poor as we are and would understand."

Ernest Hemingway
"The Old Man and the Sea"

*H*is name was Giuseppe Paolo DiMaggio and he came from the community of Isola Delle Femmine, an islet off the coast of Sicily, where the DiMaggios had been fishermen for generations. Known as Zio Pepe, he migrated to the town of Martinez, a small fishing community some 25 miles northeast of the Golden Gate. In 1915, hearing of the luckier waters of San Francisco, he packed his fishing boat with his furniture and his family and docked at Fisherman's Wharf in San Francisco.

He found a flat on Taylor street, near the Wharf, and there he lived and worked at the sea and began to raise his large family. His children, in order, were Nellie, Mamie, Tom, Marie, Mike, Frances, Vince, Joe Jr., and Dominic. He wanted two of the boys to help him in the fish business, one to be a great opera singer, one to be a lawyer because "he wears glasses," and one to be a bookkeeper, "because you can sit down."

Instead, three of the sons went on from Fisherman's Wharf to become the greatest baseball playing family in the history of the game, one of them being the immortal Joe DiMaggio, the Yankee Clipper. In 13 years of baseball, from 1936 to 1949, this son of an immigrant fisherman earned an estimated total of $704,769 playing for the New York Yankees team.

When the elder DiMaggio came to Fisherman's Wharf from Martinez the younger Joe was only one year old. Fisherman's Wharf in those days was placid and picturesque, but there was also a competitive undercurrent and struggle for power along the pier. At dawn the boats would sail out for their catch, and then the men would race back with their hauls, hoping to beat their fellow fishermen to shore and sell it while they could. Some 20 or 30 boats would sometimes be trying to gain the channel shoreward at the same time and a fisherman had to know every rock in the water, and later, know every bargaining trick along the shore, because the dealers and some restaurateurs would play one fishermen off against the other, keeping the prices down.

In time the fishermen became wiser and organized, pre-determining the maximum amount each fisherman could catch. But, there were always some men who, like the fish, never learned and so sometimes heads would be broken, nets slashed, gasoline poured onto their fish and flowers of warning placed outside their doors.

Those days were ending when the elder DiMaggio arrived and he wanted his five sons, at first, to succeed him as fishermen. The first two did, Tom and Mike. The third, Vincent, liked to sing. He sang so well, and his fame spread in the Italian community, that the great banker A. P. Giannini heard him and offered a plan to send him to Italy for tutoring. But, there was not enough money around the DiMaggio household and they hesitated, and Vince never went. With the other boys it was different. Joe tells about it in his autobiography, *Lucky to be a Yankee:*

"I was born in Martinez, but my earliest recollection was of the smell of fish at Fisherman's Wharf, where I was brought up. Our main support was a fishing boat, with which my father went crabbing. If you didn't help in the fishing, you had to help in cleaning the boat.

"Baseball didn't have much appeal to me as a kid, but it was far better than helping Pop when he was fishing, or helping clean the boat. I was always giving him excuses, principally that I had a weak stomach, but he insisted I was 'lagnuso' (lazy) and to tell you the truth, I don't know which he thought was the greater disgrace to the family, that a DiMaggio should be lazy or that a DiMaggio should have a weak stomach.

"There was a lot of us DiMaggios, nine in all. Pop worked on a two-year scale and everybodys clothes fit everybody else, which meant that only Nellie, the oldest girl, and Tom, the oldest boy, ever got a chance to wear new clothes. Hand-me-downs outfitted the rest of us. Pop didn't like baseball in those days. 'Too many shoes, too many pants,' was his description of our national pasttime. Even with plenty of hand-me-downs, the DiMaggios in those days couldn't reconcile themselves to the shoes I wore out or the pants I tore in my baseball cavorting. Bocci was pop's game, an Italian version of lawn bowling.

"Baseball to me in those days was merely an excuse to get away from the house and away from the chores of fishing. When Pop gave up trying to make me work on the boat, I gave up playing baseball in the sand patch by the Wharf, and tried my hand at selling newspapers, a job my father declared suited me perfectly since it consisted mostly of standing still and shouting.

Joe Di Maggio in Action

"Vince, who had been far more successful than I in baseball, had quit high school to help support the family, although my mother's advice was to continue his education. Two years later, I followed Vince. Up to the time my baseball playing had been sketchy. In fact, I almost stopped playing when I was 14. Our home was by Fisherman's Wharf, close to the old North Beach playground, where I had my first baseball experience at the age of ten. I was third baseman in those days and played well enough to be on the usual teams with the kids around my block.

"Pop, having despaired of my ever becoming a fisherman, urged me to study bookkeeping. 'It's a job you can do sitting down,' said Pop significantly, for he was convinced I was lazy.

"Vince, meanwhile, was making good in a big way, or so it seemed to me. He had been signed by the San Francisco Seals and farmed out to Tucson. I was a pretty cocky kid in those days and I said to myself, 'If Vince can get dough for playing ball, I can, too.' As a matter of fact, Vince often pleaded with me to take the game more seriously, and it was his idea that I could play well enough to make money at it.

"Some of the kids around the block decided to get up a team and go in the Boys Club League, and we won the championship in our division. There was an olive oil dealer in our neighborhood, named Rossi, who took our club out of the Boys Club League and outfitted us with better uniforms and equipment that we ever had before. He was a real fan and took great pride in having a ball club of his own. We won the championship in a play-off, in which I hit two home runs. As a reward for this, I received two gold baseballs and two orders for merchandise worth about $8 each. It was my first financial return from baseball."

With his brother playing for the San Francisco Seals, Joe began hanging around the ball park and to his delight was invited to the Seals training camp for the 1933 season. Joe made the team and sports writers described him as "a tall gangling youngster, all arms and legs and like a frisky colt." His batting prowess soon asserted itself and, in his first year, Joe was attacking the league record for hitting in successive games. There were 10,000 people in Seals Stadium on July 4, 1933, including Joe's family, to watch him try for a hit in his 49th straight game, which would break a long standing record. In the first inning Joe singled to center field and the record was broken.

"Then the game was stopped," Joe recalled. "Angelo Rossi, Mayor of San Francisco, came on to the field to congratulate me personally, which was quite a thrill to a kid who couldn't be able to vote for him for three more years.

"My whole family was on hand and my mother hugged me for joy. She didn't understand much about baseball but she realized I was being honored and that was enough for her. The publicity attendant on my batting streak converted Pop to baseball. At first, he thought it was silly for people to dress up in short pants, with spikes and gloves. Then he couldn't see me, a kid, making good against 'all those older men.' He forget about this and even forgot about bocci. 'Bocci ball?' Pop would say, 'No money in bocci ball. Baseball, that's the game.'"

Joe's hitting streak finally ended at 61 games. He was then presented with a watch by Mayor Rossi and a travelling bag from his friends at Fisherman's Wharf. Joe secretly was more pleased with the travelling bag.

The travelling bag came in handy because Joe was then signed for the 1936 season to play with the New York team, the start of a brilliant career that took him for the first time away from the Fisherman's Wharf he knew so well. Baseball opened many doors for Joe. At 6 feet, 2 inches, with brown eyes and black hair, he struck an impressive role both on and off the field. Joe immediately broke into cafe society and was named one of the nation's ten best dressed men. But, Joe never forgot San Francisco, nor they him. After his first season with the Yankees, Joe returned home to a hero's welcome.

"They had a brass band to meet me at the station," recalled Joe. "My parents were crying like children and everyone was shouting, 'DiMag is back.' All the fellows I'd grown up with at Fisherman's Wharf were there and they hoisted me on their shoulders and took me to an automobile which carried me to City Hall. There, Mayor Rossi made a speech of welcome, telling me how much I'd done for San Francisco. If I were any kind of a speaker then, which I was not, I could have told the Mayor that San Francisco had done a lot for me, too."

While Joe was beginning to hit home runs and break more records, the third DiMaggio, this one Dominic, was making his way up the same baseball ladder. He was the smallest and youngest of the DiMaggios. "I was determined to become a big leaguer," said Dom, "to disprove all those cracks that I was being given my start just because of my brothers." Wrote one cruel sports writer: "He is the tail on Joe's kite." Dom was named "most valuable" player on the Seals and in 1940 went to the Boston Red Sox where he was known as the "Little Professor." He soon moved out of Joe's deep shadows, which blanketed him in his early years, and ran up an impressive record of his own.

"I think Pop's pride and joy was Dom," said Joe. "When Dominic was in short pants, Pop wanted him to become a lawyer because 'he wears glasses.' Dom, who never looked as though he'd grow to be five feet, gained about five inches in his 18th year and promptly turned to baseball. As a purely personal opinion, I think he's the best defensive outfielder I've ever seen."

Dominic fished more than either of his baseball brothers, Vince or Joe. He enjoyed the clear moonlit nights, the easy motions of the fishing boat and the harvest of fish that poured from the nets. He often went out with his brother Mike and on one occasion had a near brush with tragedy.

"Mike and I were out this one night," said Dominic, "It was rough and choppy. We had a net out and were rounding a point. Usually the current took us out. This time it carried us in. We never learned why. There was a reef off the point, with just a narrow passage between it and the mainland. Our only choice was to squeeze through. Just as we reached it, Mike cut the net loose, and in we went. There was a strong current. The water came up to the gun'les and we scraped bottom, but we went through. If we'd ever hit or stuck—well, we lost the net, but saved our lives."

Tragedy later struck down Mike in 1953, at the age of 44, when he fell from his boat while fishing in the Bay and drowned.

By now Joe and the DiMaggio family were national celebrities. The elder DiMaggio was always being greeted on the Wharf by friends and strangers alike, who wanted to talk baseball. With three of his sons in baseball Zio Pepe learned enough of the game to carry on conversations about batting averages and who was going to win the pennant.

Zio Pepe developed an uncanny sense of prophecy about Joe's game. In 1938, he predicted Joe would hit 46 home runs, which he did. Joe crossed him up in 1940. The elder DiMaggio called for 30 home runs, and Joe hit 31. Joe went on to many baseball records. He led the American League in batting in 1939 and 1940 and led in the number of home runs in 1937 and 1948. He batted safely in 56 consecutive games in 1941 for a new record, and he was named the most valuable player in the American League in 1939, 1941 and 1947.

If there was any doubts of Joe's role as a celebrity outside of the playing field they were dispelled on November 19, 1939, when he married movie actress Dorothy Arnold, whom he met while making a movie in Hollywood. The ceremony was held at St. Peter and Paul Church in North Beach and some 30,000 persons crowded the church inside and outside to see the famed couple. Fans climbed trees and stood on rooftops to catch a glimpse of the couple leaving the church.

With the baseball DiMaggio's earning more money than any fisherman ever dreamed, Joe first bought a new home for his folks in the Marina District, and still comfortably near the Wharf. In 1937, the DiMaggio's decided to open a restaurant on the Wharf, called "Joe DiMaggio's Grotto," and the huge electric sign showed Joe in his familiar baseball hitting stance. The walls of the restaurant itself were lined with pictures of Joe's and Dom's and Vince's baseball buddies. Tom took over the management of the restaurant and it proved an excellent opportunity for the older DiMaggio to retire gracefully from fishing.

The elder DiMaggio took great pride in preparing meals for baseball players who visited the Grotto during the off season. He often cooked them the Italian dish of cioppino, gave them towels for bibs and told them to dig in with fingers, no knives or forks permitted.

Divorce came to Joe and Dorothy Arnold in 1944, and then came his much publicized romance and marriage to film actress Marilyn Monroe in January of 1954. They were married at City Hall in San Francisco and reporters stood on chairs to look over the transom at the judge performing the ceremony. Joe brought Marilyn to live with him in a home near the Wharf in San Francisco. Sometimes they could be seen early in the morning, fishing off Joe's boat, the *"Yankee Clipper."* In the evening they could be seen walking along the pier, holding hands and passing by many tourists who failed to recognize the famed couple. Columnists took delight in writing about Marilyn shopping in neighborhood stores and not being recognized.

But all was not rosy. Joe was then 39, and Marilyn, 27, and there was to be a growing disharmony in their temperaments. Joe had been through his baseball career and he was tired of publicity, while Marilyn was thriving on it. Joe was intolerant of tardiness, while Marilyn was always late. In a much repeated story, Marilyn appeared before some 10,000 troops in Korea to entertain and later exclaimed to Joe: "You never heard such cheering!" and Joe replied, "Yes, I have."

They separated nine months after their marriage and were later divorced. Marilyn later married, and divorced, playwright Arthur Miller. But after Marilyn's death it was a sorrowful Joe who made the funeral arrangements. He described Marilyn as a "warmhearted girl that those people in Hollywood took advantage of."

In time, Joe sold out his interest in the family restaurant, though he was seen there on many occasions over the years. He invested his money wisely and took part in a number of business deals. He returned to baseball in 1968 as a coach for the newly transferred Oakland Athletics. Vince, who played on a number of major league teams, retired to live and work as a carpenter in nearby Pittsburg, California. Dom became the most successful in the business world and went to live in a fashionable Boston suburb with his family.

Chapter 19

BARNEY GOULD'S SHOWBOAT

*T*he invasion of San Francisco's shores by Captain Fremont in 1848 drew little attention compared to the public furor created by another invasion more than 100 years later by Captain Barney Gould and his showboat at the shores off Fisherman's Wharf.

Barney Gould was a handsome, cherubic character who wanted to be an actor, playwright and theatrical producer. Instead, fate forced him to be a reporter, press agent and sportswriter. Barney, a native Californian, began to dream of his idea of a show boat to perform oldtime minstrel shows back in the 1930s when he attended Stanford University, where he was editor of the *"Chaparral,"* the university humor magazine, and a writer and actor in Stanford theatricals. After graduation from Stanford in 1931, Barney took on a variety of activities.

He became editor of the San Francisco *News Letter and Wasp*, the West's oldest weekly, wrote drama criticism for the Hollywood *Reporter*, went to Hollywood and did some comedy script writing and later helped organize the Los Angeles Newspaper Guild. In 1934, Barney spent the summer in Sacramento performing in the perennial play, *"The Drunkard,"* and between shows spent time at the library studying early California theatrical history. Between 1935 and 1938, he found time to produce a few shows and the idea of his show boat grew stronger.

Barney had observed with regret the passing of the famous paddlewheel packets which plied between San Francisco Bay and the Sacramento and San Joaquin Rivers. They were the Far Western counterparts of the Mississippi tradition. The Argonauts of the great Gold Rush reached the Mother Lode country mostly by river steamer. Crude theatres and music halls were established to entertain miners. The idea of combining the 100-year-old river boat tradition of California and adding the theatrical show boat lore to the color of the Gold Rush was burning in Barney's fertile mind.

In 1939, Barney first proposed his idea of Western showmanship to officials of San Francisco's World Fair at Treasure Island, built in the middle of the Bay and ideal for Barney's purpose. The resources were already docked there in the presence of the riverboat *Fort Sutter,* which was then being used as a floating barracks for Works Progress Administration theatre personnel performing at the World's Fair. Little did those officials, or even Barney for that matter, realize the spectacular and historical role that same *Fort Sutter* was to play in later years.

Be that as it may, the World's Fair officials turned Barney down cold. There is no claiming that Barney's idea would have solved everyone's financial problems, but the 1939 Fair turned out to be an artistic success, and a financial failure. City officials and private backers, seeking to recoup their losses, came back for more in May of 1940 and re-opened the World's Fair. In the beginning, things went even worse than the previous year. But help came from an unexpected source, the same Barney Gould. He wangled for the Fair one of the all-time money makers in show business, the fabulously successful Billy Rose and his "Aquacade," and when the exposition finally closed in September it ended up with an operating profit of nearly $1,000,000.

At the close of World War II, Barney found the opportunity to bring his Showboat idea closer to reality. During the war he had proposed a showboat-style Stage Door Canteen and it was to be anchored at the Ferry Building. The idea was rejected, again, and instead Barney was relegated to helping Ina Claire establish the Canteen on dry land in the Native Sons Hall. With the conclusion of hostilities, all the Bay Area ferries and riverboats used as floating barracks by the armed forces were declared to be surplus. This was Barney's opportunity and in March, 1947, he took the bold step of buying the old 741-ton sternwheeler *"Capitol City"* for $4,000 and tied her up at the ferry slip at the foot of Hyde Street, hard by Fisherman's Wharf.

Permission was granted by the Board of State Harbor Commissioners to operate there the West's first showboat. But, came the first of many disillusionments for Barney. Many prominent businessmen who had promised Barney financial aid, did not come through. The boat lay idle and dock fees of $250 a month began piling up.

Barney saw a ray of hope in 1949 with the Gold Rush Centennial ceremonies, in which he joined as managing director. The centennial celebration was spread over a three year period and Barney proposed his Showboat promotion to the directors. They were not interested.

Meanwhile, the gallant *"Capital City"* rode the waves impatiently at the Hyde Street Pier. As the bill for fees grew, the Port Authority tired of waiting for payment and moved the boat to the ignominious out of the way resting place at the Sixth Street Channel. Disaster struck during the heavy March storms of 1952. The *"Capital City"* broke loose from its mooring and a tug called to help out nudged the sternwheeler into a piling, which tore a 40-foot hole in her hull. She promptly sank in 20 feet of water.

A bitter and disgusted Barney rowed publicly with the Port Authority, the first of Barney's many fights with hard-headed government officials. Barney said the Port Authority sent the tug on its own and was liable for damages. The Port Authority said the tug was called by Barney. After months of long and fruitless debate the State finally had the boat dismantled into scraps of lumber and hauled away.

Barney watched silently as cranes batter his Showboat into meaningless pieces of lumber. Five years of owning a Showboat, and 22 years of planning crumbled away before his very eyes. Barney decided this time he needed more direct action. He found it in the 1139-ton four-decker *Fort Sutter,* by then one of the last remaining riverboats and a familiar friend he recalled from World's Fair days. Used as a floating barracks during the war, she later served as a hotel and restaurant at a fishing resort near Rio Vista, 80 miles from San Francisco, up the Sacramento River. It was there that Barney found her and with financial helpers acquired the boat for $12,000. He was on his way.

Barney went to the City's Park and Recreation Commission and got permission to bring in a "historic river boat at Aquatic Park, next to the Maritime Museum." The Commission later said they assumed the boat would be a part of the Museum. The Museum later said they assumed otherwise. Anyway, early on the morning of February 13, 1953, which noticeably fell on a Friday, Barney brought his *Fort Sutter* boat into Aquatic Park. Bad timing with the high tide left the *Fort Sutter* resting on a sand shoal 75 feet from the sea wall. The next day, at precisely high tide, with tractors on shore helping out,

Barney guided his boat towards land. He was nattily attired for the occasion in a semi-nautical garb of blue denim slacks, bright red sweater and white cap. The natty attire was soon rumpled when a line was tossed from the boat to shore. Barney failed to catch it, so he had to wade into the water up to his neck to retrieve the line. A crowd of some 500 on shore, attracted by the pre-publicity fanfare, cheered Barney on.

Captain Barney, a title firmly tagged on by newspapers, finally stood aside and watched his creation safely anchored in the sands.

"Let 'em try to stop me now," said Barney triumphantly to nearby reporters. "Within 60 to 90 days she'll be in operation," he said. Barney told eager reporters of his plans to convert the craft into a dining-dancing-theatrical showboat. He estimated it would cost almost $100,000 to convert the ship into his dreams.

But, if Barney thought his only trouble was to round up $100,000 cash, he soon learned otherwise. Immediately, a storm of civic protest broke out and from the shore batteries of three nearby private rowing clubs came thunderous blasts of complaint. The City was "hoodwinked" they complained. The ship was described as "an eyesore and a booze ship." Nearby merchant groups gathered petitions to ask why Barney should be allowed to beach his craft on a public beach. "It's unsightly and it spoils the beach," they said.

The nearby South End Rowing Club called for a public hearing of protest, to which Barney was not invited. He went anyway. Barney barged through the door while the meeting was in progress. He sailed his hat against the wall and marched to a front row seat amid a chorus of boos. Speaker after speaker arose to call the boat "a derelict, an eyesore, a monstrosity, an obscenity and a filthy rotten hulk."

"If you want a fight, you'll get a fight!" shouted Barney and he rose to speak, but was gavelled down. "This is America, not the Kremlin!" Barney roared. Finally, the chairman called for a vote and it was agreed Barney could speak.

Barney defended his boat and said it would bring much revenue to the City in taxes. He caustically termed the meeting "a minority group who think they can dictate public policy, while using public facilities for private gain." Barney was right. The rowing club, with two others, was leasing its clubhouses from the City for very small rentals.

"It will take an act of Congress to remove the boat," said Barney boldly as he finished. Going out the door, Barney added: "And I'll start painting the boat to-morrow!"

"Save your money," came a voice from the side.

"Save your voice!" Barney yelled back.

The civic protests began to mount. The City's chief health inspector made an un-official visit to the beach and said the *Fort Sutter* "has a bellyful of rats." Barney fired back: "I don't know but the rats arrived after the boat did. They may have come from the nearby rowing clubs."

A Citizens Committee was formed to "remove this horrible blight from Aquatic Park." Chairman Francis Carroll charged that "not even personable promoter Gould should be permitted to take this small public beach for his personal profit."

Barney easily brushed off Carroll. "Such protests are old tricks for Carroll," said Barney. "He used to object to my singing in the shower at Toyon Hall at Stanford." For other purposes, Barney added: "Their statements are maliciously untrue and they will be called to account for such inflamatory adjectives."

The protest, however, had their effect and two weeks after Barney beached his boat the Park and Recreation Commission, with authority over the public beach, called for a public hearing. A standing room only crowd jammed the commission hearing room.

"The debate was enlivened by shouting theatrics, bitter insults and moderated by an occasional calm discussion," reported the *Chronicle*.

The opposition fired thunderous blasts against Barney. "We don't want a saloon on the beach." Others described the vessel in nightmarish terms: "That old, rotten, rat-infested and dilapidated boat . . ." Another argued "Restore the beach to the citizens."

An old time thespian defended Barney. "I think the showboat is a wonderful idea," he said. "God bless Barney for what he's done for us." Another friend likened the attacks as ridiculous as "tearing down the Parthenon."

Then Barney rose to speak. He planted himself firmly, feet slightly apart.

"I hope to be of somewhat higher caliber than those of the barroom brawlers arranged against me," he began. Boos and catcalls were the answer.

"My opponents are a couple of private rowing clubs, a few Fisherman's Wharf restaurant owners and Russian Hill view monopolists. They have often been selfish or short-sighted opposition to public projects for the good of San Francisco."

The furor was too much for the Commission and they scheduled a second hearing, which was just as emotional. Fire and health authorities were skeptical of Barney's plans. Others testified the decks were sagging.

Barney started speaking again:

"Like the richly remembered Cross of Gold speech by William Jennings Bryan. . ."

He was interrupted by cries of "Oh, no." Others taunted him with "we want Shakespeare!" Commission President Louis Sutter rapped for order and Barney continued . . .

". . . Bryan, speaking in his own prime of life, said 'the humblest citizen in all the land, when clad in the armor of righteous cause, is stronger than all the hosts of error'."

After two weeks of thinking, the Commission came up with their version of a compromise. They ruled Barney had to move off the beach, but gave him the right to dock at nearby Van Ness Avenue pier. This caused Barney trouble with his backers, Tom Anderson and W. O. Wheeler, who were tiring of the delays and controversy. Wheeler announced he was backing out. Anderson went to court for a writ to prevent Barney from moving—he wanted to move it himself. Barney didn't like that, figuring Anderson would keep sailing the boat to another city. He got his own writ and confronted Anderson on board ship, with a police escort, and the usual press corps.

"If we can't refloat the *Fort Sutter* we're going to sue San Francisco," growled Anderson.

"Why San Francisco?" he was asked.

"Because Barney controls the police department," complained Anderson. "Well, I'm glad to hear that," said a surprised Barney.

Barney then reluctantly began his own plans of moving the boat, which was not easy if you have ever tried to move a 1139-ton ship off a beach. Weeks passed. The impatient City ordered Barney to move "at the next high tide." The tide ebbed and flowed and nothing happened.

"We want that boat off the beach," the City warned.

"Wishing won't get it off," complained Barney.

Deadlines and threats followed threats and deadlines by the City. The boat was becoming a civic headache so when December 1953 came along and Barney finally found new financial backing, why it became front page news. It was though the City was shouting in relief.

Thousands lined the beach on Sunday, December 20, as tugs and bulldozers came and huffed and puffed— without success. Thousands came the next day, and the next. Finally, the tugs pulled her off the sands, as an estimated crowd of 5,000 cheered. The boat moved out into the water, after 10 months of controversy. The City commissioners wiped their brows in relief. It was all premature.

The boat was tugged some 150 yards off shore, but she began taking water in alarming amounts and frantic tug operators ran her back on the beach, just 100 yards from the spot she had just left!

Now the *Fort Sutter* was beached again, and there she was to remain over an embattled period of six more years. When news was quiet, newspapers would editorially complain about the boat. The City periodically ordered Barney to "forthright move the boat." Barney periodically mentioned possible new backers. The Board of Supervisors voted $30,000 to move the boat off the beach, but the new Mayor George Christopher vetoed the appropriation. "I don't think we should pay for the mistakes of a previous administration," he said.

Rats and teredo worms began to take their toll of the hull of the *Fort Sutter*. In 1957, the desperate Park and Recreation asked the fire department to burn the boat. The fire department said no, thanks.

Then on the night of May 1, 1959, the problem was solved. In a mysterious attack that has never been explained, four youths drove up in a car in the middle of the night, poured gasoline on the deck of the boat and set it afire in a spectacular blaze. A night watchman on deck came running up, too late. He was trapped by the quick spreading flames and rescued by firemen.

Barney Gould himself came rushing to the scene, sat dejectedly on the shore and bemoaned the fates that saw the second of his showboats destroyed. Barney went home and his anger and bitterness grew. He brushed aside editorials of the *Sacramento Union* which had been conducting a campaign to secure the *Fort Sutter* for exhibition at the Embarcadero of the State Capitol. Barney then wrote a public statement addressed, "To Whom It May Concern:"

"While our ostrich City Hall and Maritime Museum are still secretly celebrating the cremation of the historic river steamer *Fort Sutter,* let us not gratefully give all the civic credit to those merry murderous arson agents who at last carried out the City's seven-year standing invitation to incendiarism."

Barney had harsh words for two different mayors and the "respectable" Park and Recreation Commission. He tore into the State Park Commission for allocating $1,000,000 to purchase three historical ships to display in San Francisco, and blithely ignoring the *Fort Sutter* as one possibility.

Barney ended with the cynical comment that he had lost to "The City That Knows How."

Chapter 20

MODERN FISHERMAN'S WHARF

Ghirardelli Square

*B*ehind the color and romanticism of Fisherman's Wharf, mecca of tourist and natives, lies the basic fact that it is a commercial business, and more fascinating and unusual than other businesses. Highlighting the unusual are some old buildings at the Wharf that have never faded away, they have been royally converted into shopping areas and glamorous office buildings. All it took was a certain flair and several million dollars for, as one builder facetiously commented, "What's a million dollars, more or less?"

This formula transformed a former chocolate factory, Ghirardelli Square, into a miniature World's Fair of shops, galleries and plazas. The square is a cluster of red brick buildings, topped by a four-story clock tower. The giant G-H-I-R-A-R-D-E-L-L-I electric sign on the roof is a carry over from the days when this was a chocolate-spice-coffee factory. Before that, the site had been a woolen mill, producing uniforms and blankets for Union Troops.

Now it caters to thousands of tourists daily who park their cars below ground, then elevate to the shops and restaurants that ring each layer of open promenade. There are boutiques for all reasons, books, flowers, gems, chairs and all sorts of clothing. This red brick fortress was

The Chocolate Makers Historic Factory

rescued from the wreckers in 1962 by William Matson
Roth, San Francisco shipping magnate, and his mother,
Mrs. Lurline Roth. They poured $5 million dollars of
their hard earned money into a magnificently successful
face lifting chore that transformed this local Wharf heir-
loom into a tourist paradise.

The man who started all this was a young chocolate
maker from Rapallo, Italy, named Domingo Ghirardelli
and he was aided and abetted by a middle age businessman
from Fredricksburg, Pennsylvania, named James Lick.
It was the same James Lick who eventually built San
Francisco's first elegant hotel, the Lick House, and en-

dowed the Lick Observatory of Mt. Hamilton. The two first met in 1847 in the most unlikely country of Peru, where the young Italian was trying to peddle his unique chocolate.

When businessman Lick sailed for San Francisco in 1847, he carried with him 600 pounds of Domingo Ghirardelli's chocolate. Domingo followed him here in 1849, one of the first Italian businessmen in California, and like so many others of that day tried his luck at mining in the Sonora area. His acumen as a miner was nil, so he pitched a general merchandise tent in downtown Stockton to become the first store owner in the town and to sweeten the teeth of local travelers with his tasty chocolate. Lick's success in San Francisco and his glowing testimonials of the chocolate sales finally brought chocolate-minded Domingo to the City by the Golden Gate. By now he had already perfected his "Broma," the early name for ground chocolate.

Domingo ultimately set his sights on the waterfront block which at that time consisted of two major buildings, the Woolen Mill, the oldest factory in the West which had been a part of Heyneman-Pick and Co., manufacturers of uniforms of the Union troops; and a wooden building called the Box Factory. The property also included a row of wooden buildings on North Point Street, which housed the workmen and their families and included stables for horses and wagons. Before he took over this square block in 1893, Ghirardelli had a chocolate factory at 415 Jackson Street and a confectionary and food shop at Kearny and Washington. Business was booming at the Kearny Street location, the center of town then and so close to the waterfront which was then at Montgomery Street, one block away.

The need to expand and to merge his warehouse operation brought Ghirardelli to the Wharf area to build his factory. The indoor courtyard was built by Ghirardelli so his employees could picnic during the lunch hour. Today this area is attractively landscaped with fruit trees, flowers and marble benches, where employees today also picnic outdoors during their lunch hour.

After he bought his wonderful piece of real estate, Domingo Ghirardelli took a trip to his native land in the following year of 1894 to see his old country friends and tell of his wonderful success story. He never returned for he died there in the town where he was born.

In the following years, the Ghirardelli heirs operated the chocolate factory and the rich smell of chocolate was a part of the scene. The massive red brick buildings, which were an important element of old San Francisco, were designed by architect William Mooser. Soon were built the chocolate building, the warehouse building, the power house, the apartment building and finally, in 1915, the handsome Clock Tower, patterned after the Chateau Blois in the Loire Valley of France. The apartment building housed the two families of the maintenance superintendents for the chocolate factory, and as recently as 1962 one of the families had been living there for more than 20 years. At one time, the Ghirardelli Chocolate Co. made spices and mustard, and one of the major brick buildings was appropriately called the "Mustard Building." The old names of the buildings have been retained in the modern shopping center.

The only building not retained by the new owners was the wooden box factory, built prior to the era of building codes in San Francisco. In its place on Beach Street is the Wurster Building, named after the architect who designed the building, William Wilson Wurster. The original drawing of the distinctive Clock Tower became the insignia for the Square. Among the many fine restaurants located there one is "Senor Pico," the first venture for Trader Vic Bergeron in early California and Mexican cookery. He named his restaurant after Pio Pico, the first Spanish governor of California whom local historians point out served only 20 days in his first term in 1832, though he did much better in his 1846 term. Modesto Lanzone's Restaurant is done in the fashion of an Italian home at the turn of the century.

The Cannery

The site of the old Del Monte Fruit Cannery at the Wharf, and why anyone needed a cannery there in the first place shows why City planners are needed, is now a magnificent three-story shopping center appropriately named The Cannery.

The shopping center has preserved the original cannery's early San Francisco exterior of weathered brick with gracefully arched doors and windows. The three-story complex is divided by a central walkway and connected at various levels by stairways, balcony arcades, bridges and a glass covered elevator. It is a beautiful environment for leisurely exploration and for dining, shopping and entertainment. You can't help seeing the Cannery at the Wharf because of its brilliant flying pennants and the main entrance which is an arched gateway under a giant five-pointed star. The central courtyard had a tinge of the Florentine renaissance and the rear courtyard is an idyllic setting that magically transforms you into a typical European setting.

The man responsible for all this is Manchurian-born Leonid Matveyeff, now known as plain Leonard Martin, a former practicing lawyer and a former law clerk to a State Supreme Court Justice. The Cannery is a one-man show because Martin has sunk $8 million of his own money into the venture and another $2.5 million he borrowed from the bank.

Martin said he got the idea for the Cannery after a sentimental trip to Europe with his wife. Why not? What else could Martin do with his idle millions?

"My wife and I were in Paris, Rome and Italy a few years ago," Martin told Columnist Herb Caen in 1969. "The atmosphere got to me—those wonderful old world places where you could stroll around between ancient walls, sit down somewhere and sip coffee, relax, and look at people. I said San Francisco needs something like this."

It was a unique interview for the Wharf and even for Caen, who has covered his share of interesting subjects. The interview took place in the kitchen at Martin's office, as Caen reported.

"Take a look at this," said Martin, opening the oven, "Siberian sturgeon pie, like my mother made. I've loved this dish since I was a kid in Harbin, Manchuria." Caen described sturgeon pie as a crusty mixture of sturgeon, salmon, long rice and finely chopped onions. It has not yet surfaced on any of the Wharf restaurant menus.

Martin acquired the cannery property and a long series of headaches. First, those imposing brick walls were not as easy to keep and restore as he thought. "I loaned a lot of money to keep two companies in business, that went out of business," said Martin of two of his early tenants. That added up to $1 million lost, he said. Those early troubles in 1969 caused a lot of rumors, like he was going broke or that the bank was going to take over. How about that rumor?

"How about it?" grinned Martin. "One of the bank's young men called me to threaten to call in the loan. I said go ahead, call it. Who's going to run a place like The Cannery? Even I'm learning! They aren't calling the loan."

How about the rumors, too, that he was selling out?

"I've heard them all," chuckled Martin. "I was even offered one price of $15 million by a Los Angeles conglomerate. I'll put it all in one sentence. The Cannery isn't going out of business. The Cannery isn't for sale. Hell, man, this is my life!"

Martin's life was quite interesting. He drove a classic battleship grey Bentley convertible whose horn played the first eight notes from "Bridge on the River Kwai." He found a 1929 New York "5th Avenue" double decker bus abandoned in a warehouse. Martin spent $30,000 to doll it up and used it as a unique shuttle service at a steady 10 mile an hour tour of the Wharf, starting at the Cannery. He worked out a widely publicized deal where musician Earl (Fatha) Hines would work there on a life time contract. Time dimmed the publicity and the unique deal.

"I'm to pay him $20,000 a year for the rest of his life," explained Martin at the time. "Of course, he has to work for it. The less he works, the less he gets. But, he wants a 16-piece band. Hell, that would cost me $60,000 a year. No chance."

Nothing topped Martin's experience than those of his penguins. Yes, for three years, 12 sleek and fun loving visitors from the Southern Hemisphere daily entertained what crowds could be induced into their small arena-stadium across the street. The Cannery's Performing Penguins, they were called. One would have to go back to the days of Abe Warner to find something as interesting.

The trained animals, 12 Humboldt penguins and a Pacific "Ocean Murre," whatever that is, were brought from their homeland off the coast of Peru because Martin wanted something different to entertain young people. In a farewell press release in 1968, describing the formal ceremonies ending the three-year experiment, this was the explanation for the presence of the 13th bird.

"He is a small Northern Hemisphere cousin who simply dropped in at the pool several days ago and decided to learn the penguin trade after he saw the uniforms, fringe benefits, and public adulation that his new-found family was enjoying," wrote preceptive Jack Wallace, a publicity man who matched anything written about the Wharf since the days of the "Cob-web Palace."

"The Murre happily joined his preceptors in today's performance, which included sports car racing, boating, surf-boarding, and a rendition of the Penguin National Anthem on the piano, all cued by trainer, young Christopher Martin and his pretty assistant, Becky Schultz."

Writer Wallace described the penguin farewell in this manner:

"In a brief ceremony this morning, at their pool on the edge of the Cannery parking lot, at Leavenworth and Jefferson Streets, the birds took time out from their merry display of musical and athletic talents to elect their own leader, Paul, as president. Paul then agreed to go along with the Establishment and relocate his troupers at the San Francisco Zoological Gardens."

The establishment was represented by Acting Mayor Peter Tamaras and Zoo Director Ronald T. Reuther, who readily accepted the penguin's offer to become wards of the City and take them off of Martin's hands. The City also accepted the penguin's apparatus, a slide, a high-dive, racetrack and electric piano. Zoo Director Reuther thanked Martin for the birds "which we thought were primitive but, as we've seen today, are really very intelligent!" Tamaras extended thanks to "The Cannery and owner Leonard Martin who has done so much to preserve and improve the color and atmosphere of the Wharf and the waterfront area."

Acting Mayor Tamaras made a big mistake. He should have thanked writer Jack Wallace!

The Man Who Plays Columbus

Every large city in America with an Italian community has an annual Columbus Day festival and the one in San Francisco is the only pageant that recreates the landing of the intrepid explorer in 1492 at San Salvador. That landing takes place at the peaceful shores of Aquatic Park, alongside the Wharf.

The man who annually plays the role of Christopher Columbus is a charming and engaging Italian by the name of Joe Cervetto, who was born in 1909 at Varazze, Savona, in Italy and emigrated here in 1933. Cervetto started playing the role of Columbus in 1951, decked out in a colorful and appropriate costume. His personality and background, and his strong Neopolitan looks and Italian accent, has made him such a carbon-copy of the original that he generally gets more publicity than anyone else.

Cervetto takes his role of Columbus quite seriously. He has read everything he could get his hands on dealing with Columbus and his travels. In 1962, while visiting Toledo, Spain, he paid $28 to have a sword forged, the same place where Columbus had his weapon made.

He purchased a 39-foot boat, which he docks in back of his substantial home on the Marina Vista Canal across the Bay in Marin County. What did he name his boat? The *"Santa Maria II,"* of course. In 1960, he paid $595 for a new costume, made of brocade, silk and gold and black velvet.

Joe came to San Francisco, in 1933, with a pocketbook that "was starving with malnutrition," but a burning ambition to succeed. After working at several odd jobs, he started the Cervetto Building Maintenance Co. in 1935 in the basement of a house on Green Street. It wasn't much of a company, the only employee being Cervetto himself. His only equipment consisted of a mop, a water pail and a pair of strong legs to carry him and his equipment to his few jobs. Today, his company employs 170 people and 20 trucks carry his equipment.

Although he worked hard and long, Joe was always busy and active in the Italian community and took over the role of Columbus in 1951.

"Many people wanted me to act funny when I put on the Columbus costume," said Joe, "but this I refuse to do. I have too much respect for the memory of Columbus to do this. To me it is a great honor to portray this man."

The news media finds him irresistible. One year, they showed him with a plastic raincoat, so as not to have the rain spoil his costume. One year, his boat couldn't make the shore, and Joe had to wade through the water. Another year, the sea was too rough and photographers showed Joe "landing" with a borrowed truck. In 1959, Joe planted his sword in the sand to signify the finding of the New World. "His sword just missed an empty Dixie cup," the reporters wrote.

Joe's worst time came in 1970 when a revolt broke

out among the band of local Indians who for seven years had joined in the ceremony by greeting Columbus when he landed on shore. The first hint of trouble had come the year before when several of the Indians as a prank knocked off Joe's hat and wig, and someone struck him in the head with a rubber tomahawk. This time the more militant of the United Bay Council of American Indians announced a boycott, growling a complaint that Columbus hadn't done any favors for the Indians and, besides, they never were invited to any of the pageant's social affairs.

The boycott announcement was made by council president, Adam Nordwall, who ran a pest control business in Hayward, and was dressed for the occasion in full Chippewa regalia with a porcupine headdress, intricate headwork and painted cheeks. Three years later the same Nordwall received international publicity by flying to Rome's airport where he drove his lance into the ground and claimed all of Italy for his Indian nation. The Italian people were so nice to him he mellowed and gave the country back before he left.

Nordwall's forthright statements in 1970 threatened to cancel the annual Columbus landing. "Columbus didn't discover America anyway," said Nordwall, "We did."

Cervetto would have none of that, and neither would his indomitable friend, Mayor Joseph Alioto. "I don't have anything against the Indians," said Cervetto, "but they can't intimidate me against the landing."

"Columbus will step ashore," the Mayor firmly announced, "and he will be fully protected and nobody will bother him." Alioto backed up his statement with a picket line of uniformed policemen. Joe Cervetto, alias Christopher Columbus, landed safely and without incident as promised—and Cervetto was on page one again.

Cervetto has been honored many times by the Italian government for his portrayal of Columbus, and his many other volunteer activities. It was for Appeals Court Justice John Molinari to best describe Joe Cervetto:

"Yes, Joe has discovered America many times, but on the other hand I am sure that America has now discovered Joe Cervetto!"

What's the Name of That Park?

Back in 1962, I was on the staff of State Senator J. Eugene McAteer to aid him in his campaign to become Mayor of San Francisco, a goal that eluded him in 1963 because of the machinations of politics and in 1967 because of a fatal heart attack. We were looking for an event to bring him publicity and our sights turned to the Wharf area at Beach and Hyde Street, that small and seemingly insignificant part of the Maritime Museum's renovation project for the area. This delightful little park with Victorian era benches and old fashioned gas lamps was so small that you could, literally, spit from one side to the other. Today it is an enchanting and romantic spot with cable cars turning around and its warmth and color makes it a delightful addition to the Wharf area.

Here then was this seemingly insignificant little park area where we set aside a Tuesday, October 16, 1962, to have a dedication ceremony. It was doubly appropriate because of McAteer's identification with his nearby Wharf restaurant. Like so many stories surrounding the Wharf, that event was to become replete with interesting problems, and a crisis or two, and to create a name controversy that probably has not been solved to this date.

We had hardly settled down to the details when we received a visit from the friendly publicist Dave Nelson, on behalf of the Maritime Museum, who wanted to know briefly "how did we get into the act?" The reality of politics took over, since it was State money being used, and ruffled feathers were smoothed with the decision that both groups would be co-sponsoring the cermony. Then we gave out with the first report and since the park had not been officially named we referred to it as "Aquatic Park," because it was located there.

We heard again from persistent Nelson who repeatedly advised us it was already being called "Maritime Plaza." When this was reported to Senator McAteer, who had commanded a destroyer in World War II, he sarcastically asked what was "Maritime" about a small plot of greenery. Then we heard from the chairman of the State Park Commission, for after all this was indeed a "State Park," who thought it should be rightfully called "Victorian Plaza," because of the obvious Victorian motif. Then we began hearing from the environmentalists of the day who thought it would be historically unique to call it "Gaslight Park."

My first inkling of the next problem came when Senator McAteer mentioned that he had tickets to the World Series, an event of great local interest because in 1962 the recently acquired San Francisco baseball Giants were in baseball's annual classic with the dreaded and powerful New York Yankees. No problem, I answered after quickly checking dates, even it it goes seven games it would be over by Sunday, and our dedication was Tuesday. The Yankees swept out in front quickly and the matter of Tuesday seemed casual in comparison to the Series.

Then came the rains to delay the series and the Giants rallied and we moved into Monday. McAteer casually announced again if the Giants won on Monday he would certainly not miss the final game of the World

Series for any ceremony. The Giants tied it at three games apiece on Monday with Billy Pierce pitching and Orlando Cepeda hitting.

What to do about the ceremony on Tuesday, what with the Army band, the Municipal Band and everyone we could invite. The solution came from a friendly Police Captain John Engler who diplomatically took an officer assigned to Candlestick Park and assigned him to the ceremony at Beach and Hyde. Immediately after the ceremony the officer naturally had to speed to his assignment in a police car to the baseball park and, naturally, he would be glad to have Senator McAteer ride with him.

Then remained the problem of how to officially name the park at the dedication. Whichever name was chosen, the other groups would be upset, and the name of the game in politics is to make friends. Without advising anyone, McAteer took to the microphone with his solution.

"With malice towards none of the names and with charity to all, I present Aquatic Park, Victorian Park, Gaslight Park and Maritime Plaza," declared McAteer. "Let posterity and San Franciscans decide what name they are to call it in the years ahead."

McAteer then sped to the final and thrilling, but sad, climax of the World Series. The Yankees won, 1 to 0, and in the last of the ninth inning Willie McCovey missed by a foot with a line drive that would have scored Matty Alou and Willie Mays with the tying and winning runs.

What's the name of the park? You can call it what you want, but if you will visit there someday you will notice two innocuous official signs with the cruelty of a bureaucratic title:

"California State Historical Maritime Park."

Bar Pilots

Every once in a while as you gaze at Alcatraz Island and the passing ships in the Bay from one of your favorite view dining rooms at the Wharf you will see a trim craft passing by with huge letters reading "PILOT." That is one of the vessels of the Bar Pilots, those hardy breed of marine navigators who guide incoming and outgoing ships safely through the harbor in all kinds of weather. Most ships have radar today as an aid in feeling their way through the fog, but those sets are not always foolproof, or maybe the operators aren't. Anyway, there must always be a bar pilot aboard and invariably they take to the bridge, complete with oilskins and sou'wester, and hunch up against the weather to look and listen, just as seamen have done through the centuries.

The ships of the Bar Pilots are always on sea patrol at their pilot station, some 11 miles outside the Golden Gate, 24 hours a day and 365 days a year. They fly a "H" pennant, an international code flag for identification. From the pilot station, pilots go aboard incoming ships (and leave outbound ones) to guide them safely in all kinds of weather, past such hazards as "Potato Patch Shoal," over the bar, through the fabled Golden Gate, and into San Francisco Bay with its treacherous tidal currents and fog.

They are a hardy breed, these bar pilots, for he must be a ships master with long experience who is appointed after rigorous examination. At times, it is strenuous work filled with risk and anxiety. When they board a ship during rough seas it can be a risky business and once aboard they take over a multi-million dollars worth of responsibility. The Bar Pilots Association was formed in 1849 by California's first legislature, who early recognized the importance of a good pilot boat system to the State's economy because fees are paid depending on the tonnage. Indeed, the Act of Pilotage was the third bill passed by the brand new legislature, following on the heels of the State Archives and State Printer bills.

The very first bar pilot was Captain William Richardson, the City's first boatbuilder, its first merchant prince, its first real estate operator and its first harbor master. The latter honor could hardly be denied him since he controlled the only boat on the Bay. Captain Richardson was an Englishman by birth who deserted as first mate from the Whaling ship *Orion,* and settled here in 1836. Captain Richardson built his boat *Ayacucho,* trained a crew, and was soon piloting vessels to anchorage in the Bay. Many of the whaleboats who entered for wood and water were taken by their one time shipmate in trade to an anchorage in a large bay across the strait north of San Francisco, now known as Richardson's Bay.

There has been some renowned schooners used by the Bar Pilots, including the unfortunate *Bonita,* whose adventures at the turn of the century was described earlier. In recent times, the *Charlene* struck a rock off the rugged Marin County coast during a dense fog—and had no problems for historians to mull over as in the case of the *Bonita.* The *Charlene* was replaced by the *Drake,* the first steel-hulled vessel ever built for the bar pilots and named after the intrepid English navigator Sir Francis Drake.

Old timers of the sea whistled in respect at the modern statistics of the *Drake,* which was designed by San Francisco naval architect L. C. Norgaard, and built in Stockton. She is 65 feet long, has a 19-foot beam and is powered by twin 400-horsepower Caterpillar diesel engines. Maximum speed is 18 knots, cruising speed 16,

and she has a 1500-gallon fuel capacity. She is equipped
with the latest in navigation aids, including radar, automatic radio direction finder, depth sounder and a full
complement of specialized radio gear. She berths eight.

Two of the other interesting ships used by the Bar
Pilots include the *California*, built in 1926 at a cost of
$140,000 under the name *Zodiac*. The other was the
Gracie S, built in 1893 and named after Gracie Spreckels,
a member of the well known California sugar and shipping family. The *Gracie S* was replaced in the mid-1940s
by the *Golden Gate*, and ended up in the hands of movie
actor Sterling Hayden. He renamed her the *Wanderer*
and sailed her on a well publicized voyage to the South
Seas that resulted in a best selling book.

Yes, We Serve Crabs!

Man and boy, Joe Tarantino has walked
and worked at Fisherman's Wharf for more than 50 years,
and his family even longer. His father, Salvatore, was
one of the most respected fish brokers of his time. He
has known the difficult times of the crab "wars,' when
crabs were sold for 5 cents each, and through the hard
times of the 1930s and later when the boardwalks at the
Wharf were replaced with paved sidewalks.

One of the true political and civic leaders of the new
Wharf, he has built two of its modern restaurants, "Tarantino's" and the "Franciscan," along with his Bell Smoked
Fish Co. He has also set the trend for political leadership
for Wharf businessmen, along with the late State Senator
Eugene McAteer, Frank Alioto as a Fire Commissioner
and William McDonnell as head of the Airport Commission.

Tarantino can remember when fish and crab were sold from fish stalls on the Taylor Street Wharf and fishermen stretched their nets on the Jefferson Street boardwalk. He can remember the changing techniques of catching crabs.

Two types of fishing gear are used to catch crabs, the hoop net and the trap. Hoop nets were used exclusively until 1939 in the northern fishery and until 1944 in the San Francisco area. Since then traps have become increasingly important until now they are used almost exclusively. The traps were woven iron frames about 36 to 44 inches in diameter, or of stainless steel mesh. Two entrance tunnels are provided on opposite sides of the trap and hinged lid covers one-half of the top. Bait is attached to the rings of the hoop nets and suspended between the tunnels of the traps.

He can remember in 1932 when bulkheads were built along Jefferson Street, defining the shoreline, and when the Aquatic Park project, designed by Arthur Brown, Jr., was built with Works Progress Administration funds. He can remember in 1935 when the trawlers moved to Eureka and in 1952 when sardines disappeared from local waters and purse seiners moved away.

Tarantino can remember Nunzio Alioto, one of the pioneers who founded "Alioto's" in 1925, and his son, Frank, the commissioner, who once drove a Cadillac with a gold crab on the hood. He knew Tomaso Castagnola, who started in 1914 and is generally credited with originating the crab cocktail. He can remember the day when fishermen cooked on twin stoves and wood for the stoves was so precious that they would lock it up for the night.

Tarantino can remember Antone Sabella, who started as a teenager selling crabs from a basket on the street

and then, in 1920, opened one of the first modern restaurants, which is now known as "Sabella-La Torre." In
1939, the Sabella family constructed a much larger and
new establishment called "A. Sabella's" on its present
site in time for San Francisco's World's Fair.

That restaurant was destroyed in a spectacular five-
alarm fire in 1964 and the modern three-story building,
which reflects the flavor of Mediterranean architecture,
was opened in 1967. The restaurant is now owned by
Lucien A. Sabella, and Lucien has been in charge since
1951, when his father died suddenly. He was for a number
of years the youngest owner of a major restaurant, frequently takes his turn in the kitchen and is today a chef
of some prominence. His son, Antone, is a graduate of
the restaurant school of training at Cornell University
and has taken his place in the restaurant.

There was Mike Geraldi, also a familiar figure at
the early Wharf with his wide basket loaded with fish for
sale. In 1935, he built the first two-story restaurant and
created the "Little Fisherman" as a symbol, a weather
beaten dour fisherman. Aside from its immense size,
the restuarant (No. 9) is identified by its Venetian gondola
mooring polls, lamp posts and booth decorations in the
old Venetian dining room.

Breaking the tradition of Italian restaurants is "To-
kyo Sukiyaki," with authentic Japanese dishes served in
an Oriental atmosphere by kimona-clad waitresses. Among
other major restaurants are "Peter Alioto's," "Castagnola's," "Di Maggio's," "Exposition Grotto," started by
Sil Oliva and his brother, Gus, who earned and lost a
million dollars in the prohibition era; "Fisherman's Grotto
No. 9," "Franciscan," where passing ships are identified
over the loud speaker system; "N. Alioto's," and "Scoma's," tucked away in a romantic setting on a commercial
pier and run by the renowned Al and Joe Scoma.

View of Modern Day Wharf
(Convention Bureau Photo)

There are many interesting attractions at the Wharf. Fishing fleet boats are for hire and sports fishing is available. Many of the boys out for a day of salmon leave just before daylight and have the unique experience of seeing the sun rise and looking behind to see the skyline and the bridges still sleeping in the dusk of a restful night.

The Red-and-White fleet, owned and operated by Harbor Tours and Albert D. Elledge, takes tourists and residents alike on a scenic tour of San Francisco Bay. There is also helicopter rides available, an attraction started by radio personality Lu Hurley.

There is "Wharfside," a one time warehouse that has come alive with distinctive charm as an office building. The main entrance features floor to ceiling murals of old Wharfside scenes. Gerson Bakar converted the old Simmons Mattress plant into a theatre-restaurant complex known as "Northpoint." Another interesting shopping center is "Cost Plus," a large warehouse full of wares of the world. There is "Ripley's Believe It or Not," and the Tommy Fong's "Wax Museum" and "Enchanted World."

There is also the famed "Calamari Club," a group of civic political and labor leaders limited to 25 in number that started by dining on the unusually specialized squid dish from which the club takes its name. Each of the members is given the nickname of a fish and, inevitably, the president became "The Kingfish." The president blows lushly on a long fisherman's horn, called "the horn of plenty," to call members to lunch. In the more than a quarter of a century of its existence, there has only been three presidents of the Calamari Club. The first was Judge Matthew Brady, who had been District Attorney for 20 years before going on the bench; Judge Clarence Morris and Judge Walter Carpeneti.

*S*an Francisco, fortunate in many ways, has been particularly fortunate in having from the early days those pioneer fishermen who ventured out the Golden Gate to fish the Bay.

These fishermen of North Beach, along with their heritage, brought back more than the magnificent salmon and the matchless crab. They brought back the indefinable magic and magnetic appeal that has become an indelible part of San Francisco's tradition and charm. Dwellers of the inner valleys, residents from the great landlocked regions, and visitors from countless foreign lands are drawn to Fisherman's Wharf by this alluring and fascinating appeal.

Fisherman's Wharf may be located in San Francisco, but indeed it belongs to all the people of America!

Chapter 21

FISHERMAN'S WHARF RECIPES

*H*ere are some of the favorite recipes of Fisherman's Wharf chefs.

Crab Ravigote

   1 pound crabmeat
   2 tablespoons chopped sweet pickle
   2 tablespoons lemon juice
  1/4 teaspoon salt
     dash pepper
   1 hard-cooked egg, chopped
   1 tablespoon chopped parsley
   2 tablespoons chopped onion
  1/4 cup mayonnaise or salad dressing
   2 tablespoons chopped stuffed olives
  1/4 tablespoon paprika
     pimiento strips

Remove any shell or cartilage from crabmeat. Combine pickle, lemon juice, seasonings, egg, parsley, onion and crabmeat. Place in 6 individual shells or on salad greens. Combine mayonnaise, olives and paprika; spread over top of crab mixture. Chill. Garnish with pimiento. Serves 6.

Crab Gumbo

  ½ pound crabmeat
  ½ cup chopped onion
  ½ cup chopped celery
  1 clove garlic, finely chopped
  ¼ cup butter or other fat, melted
  2 teaspoons salt
  ¼ teaspoon crushed whole thyme
  ¼ teaspoon sugar
  1 whole bay leaf
    dash pepper
  1 package (10 ounces) frozen okra, sliced
  2 cans (1 pound, 4 ounces each) tomatoes
1½ cups cooked rice

Remove any shell or cartilage from crabmeat. Cook onion, celery and garlic in butter until tender. Add seasonings, okra, and tomatoes. Cover and simmer for 45 minutes. Remove bay leaf. Add crabmeat; heat. Serve over rice. Serves 6.

Crab Souffle

    1 pound crabmeat
    3 tablespoons butter or other fat
    ¼ cup flour
  1½ teaspoons salt
    ½ teaspoon powdered mustard
    1 cup milk
    3 egg yolks, beaten
    2 tablespoons chopped parsley
    2 teaspoons grated onion
    1 tablespoon lemon juice
    3 egg whites, beaten

Remove any shell or cartilage from crabmeat. Melt butter; blend in flour and seasonings. Add milk gradually and cook until thick and smooth, stirring constantly.

Stir a little of the hot sauce into egg yolk; add to remaining sauce, stirring constantly. Add parsley, onion, lemon juice and crabmeat. Fold in egg white. Place in a well-greased 1½ quart casserole. Place casserole in a pan of hot water. Bake in a moderate oven, 350 degrees for 1 hour or until souffle is firm in the center. Serve immediately. Serves 6.

Crab Creole

    1 dry onion
    1 clove garlic
    3 pieces celery
       two #2 can solid pack tomatoes
       one #2 can tomato puree
       crab, in amount desired
       pinch sweet basil, laurel rosemary leaves
       few grains, cayenne, paprika
       small dash of worcestershire

Dice dry onions, garlic and celery. Saute in olive oil until
brown. Add seasoning and enough flour to thicken, then
add the tomatoes, tomato puree and herbs. Salt and
pepper to taste. Cook four hours. When ready to serve,
add crab and cook for ten minutes. Makes one quart
for serving.

Crab Canape

    1 pound fresh crabmeat, body and legs
    1 teaspoon dry English mustard
    4 ounces mayonnaise
    1 teaspoon onion powder
    1 tablespoon lemon juice
    4 slices imported Swiss cheese
    2 tablespoons grated parmesan cheese
    4 slices toasted bread

Mix together crabmeat, mustard, mayonnaise, onion powder and lemon juice. Blend well with fork and spread generously on four slices of toasted bread. Top each with a slice of Swiss cheese and sprinkle with a teaspoon of parmesan cheese.

Place in 450 degree pre-heated oven for 6 or 7 minutes, or until cheese becomes bubbly. As a canape, the toast slices may be sectioned into tid-bit size or served complete as an open faced sandwich.

Crab Cioppino

             3 tablespoons olive oil
             2 garlic buds, minced
             4 onions, chopped
             3 tablespoons parmesan cheese
             2 bay leaves
             1 tablespoon oregno
             1 tablespoon rosemary
             1 teaspoon chili powder (optional)
               salt and pepper to taste
             3 cracked crabs, either with shell or without
               a generous splash of white, dry wine

Saute garlic and onion in olive oil until golden brown.
Add parmesan cheese and mix well. Add tomatoes, herbs
and seasoning. Stir well and simmer 3 to 4 hours over
low fire. Add crab and continue to simmer for 20 minutes
and splash in wine. Serves 5 or 6.

Crab Victoria

    2 cups flaked crabmeat
    3 tablespoons butter
    3 tablespoons flour
    1 cup canned chicken broth
    ½ cup cream
    8 ounces cheddar cheese, diced
      one 4 ounce can sliced mushrooms
    3 tablespoons sherry
      salt, pepper, paprika to taste

Melt butter in top of double broiler. Stir in flour and gradually add stock and cream. Cook, stirring constantly until thick. Remove from heat and set over hot water.

Add cheese and stir until cheese melts., Add mushrooms, sherry, seasoning and crabmeat. Let stand over hot water until serving time. Serve on noodles, or toast. Serves six.

Spaghetti and Crabmeat

¼ cup olive oil
1 cup chopped onions
1 teaspoon chopped garlic
1 teaspoon chopped parsley
1 teaspoon chopped celery
1 cup solid pack tomato sauce
grated parmesan cheese
¼ cup sherry
1 teaspoon black pepper
2 teaspoons salt
½ teaspoon paprika
1½ cup water
1 pound fresh crabmeat
1 pound spaghetti

Saute onion, celery, garlic and parsley in oil until golden brown. Add tomatoes, tomato sauce, water and seasoning. Simmer over low flame for one hour. Add crabmeat and wine and simmer for 10 minutes. Cook and drain spaghetti (do not wash) and add to sauce. Place on serving platter and top with generous sprinkling of parmesan cheese. Serves 5 to 6.

Stuffed Turbot with Deviled Crab

             6 filets of turbot
             ½ pound cooked crabmeat

Saute the following ingredients in sauce pan:

             2 medium sliced mushrooms
             ½ clove of crushed garlic
             1 clove chopped shallots
             ½ diced pimiento
                chopped parsley
             ½ oz. of flaming brandy
             2 oz. Sherry wine
                add ½ cup of basic American white sauce
             1 egg
                dash of tobasco sauce
             4 drops worcestershire sauce
                salt and pepper to taste

Cook for 10 minutes. Remove from fire and place in refrigerator until firm. (Yield 2 servings.)

Step #2. Make a long cut down the back of the turbot and detach the filets from the backbone as you filet any of the flounder family type.

Step #3. In a well buttered fish poaching pan place 2 pieces of turbot. Put about 4 oz. of the deviled crab on top of each filet and proceed to make the turbots by interlocking 2 filets on top of the deviled crab, rolling them with your hands firmly so they will not come apart while cooking.

Step #4. Now the turbot is ready for the oven. Pour 1 cup of sherry wine over turbots and salt lightly. Sprinkle paprika and drawn butter over each turbot and garnish with a slice of lemon. Bake in oven of 400 degrees for 20 to 25 minutes, basting frequently.

Serve in hot casserole with baked potato and zucchini Milananaise.

Salmon Broccoli Pie

      1 pound can salmon
     ¼ cup butter or margarine
     ¼ cup flour
     ½ teaspoon thyme
     ¼ teaspoon pepper
      2 cups salmon liquid and milk
      1 can (4 ounces) chopped mushrooms, drained
      1 tablespoon chopped parsley
    1½ cups cooked, drained, chopped broccoli
      1 cup pastry mix

Drain salmon, reserving liquid. Break salmon into large pieces. Melt butter; blend in flour and seasonings. Add salmon liquid gradually and cook until thick and smooth, stirring constantly. Add mushrooms, parsley, and salmon.

Spread broccoli in a 9-inch pie pan. Pour salmon mixture over broccoli. Prepare pastry mix as directed. Roll dough to form a 10-inch circle. Place dough over salmon mixture. Double edge of pastry over and pinch with fingers to make an upright rim. Cut top to allow steam to escape. Bake in a hot oven, 425 degrees for 20 to 25 minutes until brown. Serves 6.

Salmon Burgers

1 pound can salmon
½ cup chopped onion
¼ cup butter or other fat, melted
1/3 cup salmon liquid
1/3 cup dry bread crumbs
2 eggs, beaten
¼ cup chopped parsley
1 teaspoon powdered mustard
½ teaspoon salt
½ cup dry bread crumbs
6 round buttered buns
lemon wedges

Drain salmon, reserving liquid. Flake salmon. Cook onions in butter until tender. Add salmon liquid, crumbs, egg, parsley, mustard, salt and salmon.

Mix well. Shape into 6 cakes and roll in crumbs. Place cakes in a heavy frying pan which contains about ⅛ inch of fat, hot but not smoking. Fry at moderate heat. When cakes are brown on one side, turn carefully and brown the other side. Cooking time, about 5 to 8 minutes. Drain on absorbent paper. Place cake in buns. Serve with lemon wedges. Serves 6.

Salmon Southern Cornbread

    1 can (7¾ ounces) salmon
    1 cup sifted flour
    1 cup cornmeal
    4 teaspoons baking powder
    ¼ cup sugar
    ½ teaspoon salt
    1 egg, beaten
    1 cup salmon liquid and milk
    ¼ cup butter or other fat, melted

Drain salmon, reserving liquid. Flake salmon. Sift together flour, cornmeal, baking powder, sugar and salt. Combine egg, salmon liquid and butter. Add to dry ingredients and mix enough to moisten. Stir in salmon. Place in a well-greased baking dish. Bake in a hot oven, 425 degrees, for 25 to 30 minutes. Serves 6.

Lobster Thermidor

    3 boiled lobsters
    2 tablespoons butter or other fat
    2 tablespoons flour
    ½ teaspoon salt
  1½ teaspoons powdered mustard
    3 teaspoons worcestershire sauce
    ¼ onion (white or green)
      dash cayenne pepper
    1 cup coffee cream
    1 can (4 ounces) mushroom stems
      and pieces, drained
      grated parmesan cheese
      dash of egg shade coloring

Split lobsters lengthwise and remove meat. Clean shells
and rinse. Cut lobster meat into ½ inch pieces. Add cream
gradually and cook until smooth, stirring constantly. Add
mushrooms and lobster meat. Blend mustard and worces-
tershire sauce. Chop onions finely and braise in melted
butter. Add flour and seasoning. Place in shells. Sprinkle
with cheese and paprika. Place on a cookie sheet. Bake
in a hot oven, 400 degrees for 10 minutes or until brown.
Serves 6.

Lobster Stew

¾ pound cooked lobster meat
1 teaspoon salt
¼ teaspoon paprika
   dash white pepper
   dash nutmeg
¼ cup butter or margarine, melted
1 pint milk
1 pint coffee cream
   chopped parsley

Cut lobster meat into ½ inch pieces. Add seasoning and lobster meat to butter; heat. Add milk and cream and bring almost to boiling point. Garnish with parsley sprinkled over the top. Serves 6.

Stuffed Swordfish

>   2 center slices swordfish
>   1 cup shrimp
>   ½ cup chopped onion
>   2 cups milk
>   dash cayenne
>   pinch dry mustard
>   chopped parsley
>   4 tablespoons melted butter
>   4 tablespoons flour
>   1 tablespoon worchestershire
>   2 oz. sherry wine
>   ¼ cup chopped pimiento

Saute onions. Add shrimps and vegetables. Cook 5 minutes. Add 2 cups milk, then remainder of ingredients. Bring to boil. Mix with rue of salt, pepper, flour and butter.

Take two center slices of swordfish, roll deviled shrimp inside. Bake 20 minutes until shrimp is hot.

Place in casserole. Cover with sauce supreme made with basic white sauce, adding 4 drops of tabasco sauce, 1 cup clam broth, 1 oz. white wine. Garnish with chopped pimiento and grated cheese. Bake 20 minutes.

Calamari Saute Picata
(Squid) Italian Style

Instructions for cleaning squid—

1. Cut head off below the eye level, towards the legs.
2. Disjoint head portion from body and discard.
3. Clean body by removing outside skin.
4. Split body down one side only and remove jelly like bone in center, and other loose material.
5. Wash thoroughly and refrigerate until ready for cooking.

Sauce

Use ½ pound of cleaned Calamari
2 large button mushrooms, sliced
1 green onion
½ clove garlic, chopped fine
pinch of parsley
¼ diced fresh tomato, peeled
1 oz. sherry wine
½ oz. lemon juice
salt to taste

Score squid by making several light cuts in square patterns, not too deep—with tip of a sharp knife. Heat 2 tablespoons olive oil in saute pan, add mushrooms, onions and cook until onions are transparent. Add squid, garlic and tomato—then parsley.

Reduce heat and cook to completion—3 to 5 minutes. Drain oil from pan. Turn up heat and add sherry and flame. Add lemon juice; simmer for 2 minutes and serve. Serve calamari on a bed of rice.